MURDER
OR
MAYHEM?

Benedict Arnold's
New London, Connecticut
Raid, 1781

by Dr. Walter L. Powell

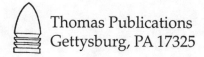
Thomas Publications
Gettysburg, PA 17325

Printed and bound in the United States of America

Published by   THOMAS PUBLICATIONS
                 P.O. Box 3031
                 Gettysburg, Pa. 17325

ISBN-1-57747-059-1

Cover design by Ryan C. Stouch

To all those who have dedicated their efforts to preserving the memory of the New London Raid — and in preserving its legacy for the future.

CONTENTS

Preface 4

New London, 1775–1781 7

The Burning of New London 24

The Battle of Groton Heights 43

The Strange Death of Col. William Ledyard 60

Appendix 71

Notes 76

Bibliography 85

PREFACE

One of the most tragic moments of the American Revolution occurred with the attack on Fort Griswold on September 6, 1781, by British soldiers from "Traitor Arnold's Murdering Corps." This attack, the bloody conclusion of General Benedict Arnold's raid on New London and Groton, resulted in the deaths of over half the defenders of Fort Griswold, including its commander, Colonel William Ledyard.

Aside from the local impact of the tragedy, the raid proved of little military importance, for the events here were overshadowed a month later by the British surrender at Yorktown. However, the raid tragically demonstrated the bloodiest aspects of a conflict which was, in many respects, America's first civil war. Half of Arnold's soldiers were Loyalists, including some from Connecticut, and their presence here enraged their former countrymen. It is not surprising, then, that the events in New London were but a few days in the past when charges of atrocity were leveled against the Loyalists, particularly for the "murder" of Colonel Ledyard and much of the garrison, and the unnecessary destruction and looting of Groton and New London.

A figure that looms large in any discussion of the New London Raid is Benedict Arnold. Born and raised in nearby Norwich, Arnold was thoroughly familiar with New London and Groton, where he had many former friends and business partners. He had been in British uniform almost a year when General Henry Clinton chose him to lead the expedition, but until that time he had seen little action. This would prove to be his last military command. What compelled

Arnold to push for this assignment is perhaps a question better left to the dramatist than the historian, for barring the discovery of more contemporary documents, Arnold's motives must be left to informed speculation. One biographer, Willard Wallace, maintained in his book *Traitorous Hero: The Life and Fortunes of Benedict Arnold*, that Arnold "showed little personal animus in the raid, and viewed the assignment as just another military command, to be executed with all his customary zeal." Based on my research I tend to agree, but notwithstanding all Arnold's efforts to spare certain property and limit the destruction, he must bear the final responsibility for all that happened. His conduct at New London must give added truth to the assertion by recent biographer James Kirby Martin (*Benedict Arnold, Revolutionary Hero: An American Warrior Reconsidered*) that "the vividly contrasting, even haunting images of the luminescent hero and the serpentine villain remain."

This study, completed as a master's thesis at Kent State University more than twenty years ago, was the first major effort in nearly a century to examine in detail the events of September 6 in light of new manuscript sources, especially the papers of Governor Jonathan Trumbull at the Connecticut State Library, and the British Headquarters Papers of Sir Henry Clinton in the Clements Library of the University of Michigan. The information contained in those sources was largely unavailable to the authors of the only two significant works published on the New London Raid in the nineteenth century: Francis M. Caulkins' *History of New London* (1852) and William Harris' *The Battle of Groton Heights* (1870), revised and enlarged by Charles Allyn in 1882. Surprisingly, these books have remained the source works for nearly all the more recent accounts of the tragedy, with the notable exception of *September 6, 1781: North Groton's Story* (New London: 1981) by Carolyn Smith and Helen Vergason, an excellent book produced for the Bicentennial and now out of print.

Like any author, I am humbled by the knowledge that the effort that went into these pages, both as a master's thesis and in its current form, is due to the kind help of many people.

While a graduate student at Kent State University, I had the pleasure to work with Dr. John Hubbell of the History Department, who served as my thesis advisor, and gave me much needed criticism and encouragement. Bruce Egli, a close friend and respected member of the Company of Military Historians, reviewed the manuscript and shared with me his substantial knowledge of 18th century fortifications and field tactics, enabling me to make better sense of my findings on the state of the fortifications and the manner in which the attack was made. On several visits to Fort Griswold State Park in 1974-75, Mr. Lloyd Whitman, then Curator, conducted me on a lengthy personal tour of the grounds and graciously provided me with all the materials he had on the events of September 6, 1781. This tradition of courtesy and helpfulness has been a benchmark for all Mr. Whitman's successors, including Mr. Jonathan Lincoln, current site manager.

During the course of several research trips, the staffs at the Connecticut State Library, the Connecticut Historical Society, and the Clements Library of the University of Michigan were especially helpful. Ms. Phyllis Kihn, former editor of The Connecticut Historical Society Bulletin, and Dr. Christopher Bickford, former director of the Society, helped me locate documents in the Society's collections and made it possible for me to examine Colonel Ledyard's vest and shirt. Ms. Kihn encouraged me to submit the early results of my research on "The Strange Death of Colonel William Ledyard" for publication in the April 1975 issue of *The Connecticut Historical Society Bulletin*. Mr. Douglas W. Marshall, then map curator, and Dr. John Dann, then curator of manuscripts at the Clements Library, provided me helpful access to the Henry Clinton papers. Most recently, members of the Friends of Fort Griswold, an organization dedicated to the preservation and interpretation of the site, have extended to me every courtesy and made available new information on current developments at the Fort.

Finally, I could not have completed this project without the love and support of my family, friends, and the wonderful staff at Thomas Publications. To all of them, this publication truly belongs.

New London,
1775-1781

During the Revolution the chief seaport of Connecticut was New London.[1] In 1774, merchants in the town employed seventy-two sailing ships and twenty smaller coastal vessels, with imported goods valued at 150-160,000 British pounds sterling, and exports at some 70,000 pounds. It was Connecticut's major trading outlet for a rich diversity of agricultural products, including wheat, rye, oats, Indian corn, flax, beans, potatoes, and beef, pork and other livestock.[2]

New London's excellent harbor was the major reason for its commercial importance. With the Thames River opening directly on Long Island Sound, there were no extensive shoals or chains of islands to obstruct the passage of ships, and during the Revolution, it became the only naval station of significance between Newport, Rhode Island and New York. The British gathered thorough intelligence on the harbor, and a survey undertaken by Major Patrick Ferguson (of King's Mountain fame) in May 1779 provides one of the best contemporary descriptions:

> The entrance of the river is formed by an Obtuse angle of low land on the west, upon the Point of which is a Lighthouse, about a mile and a half inland from which the Land begins to rise, where the Town begins—on the East side there is a low

point and reef. The river is 1 1/2 miles wide the first 3 miles, three miles further half as much, Six miles from the Entrance there is water for Ships of the Line, but then there is a bar...and no craft can ascend...Norwich landing...Three miles from the entrance there is an inlet called the Cove where Vessels drawing 10' can enter at low water, and the anchorage and Shelter are Excellent.[3]

With the outbreak of war in April 1775, New London, which once had led Connecticut in peacetime commerce, now became the state center for wartime naval activity. Most notably, the harbor became a haven for privateers, whose activities dwarfed those of the small Continental Navy, and the various state navies. These vessels, licensed by Congress or the states to attack enemy ships, held out the lure of shorter terms of service and the prospect of prize money. Many prominent local businessmen financed their construction, including Edward Hallam, Joseph Packwood, and John Deshon of New London, and Thomas Mumford of Groton. The largest local concern was Nathaniel Shaw, Jr. and Company, owned by New London's wealthiest and most prominent merchant, who was also a leading authority on naval affairs. Nathaniel Shaw owned and operated ten armed vessels during the war, in addition to his merchant ships.[4]

Several ships of reputation were constructed in New London, and the success of their cruises marked the town for future British reprisals. One of these vessels, the *General Putnam*, was considered the fastest sailer in New England. Built by Nathaniel Shaw and commissioned in April 1778, the *General Putnam* captured over fourteen British vessels. Her career was cut short when she was destroyed in the ill-fated Penobscot, Maine expedition in August 1779.[5] Another of Shaw's vessels, the *American Revenue*, captured thirteen British ships between 1778-1779.[6] The success of many individual cruises such as these prompted Admiral George Collier, Commodore of the British fleet in New England waters from 1776-1779, to write: "The place was a famous receptacle for Privateers, and was thought on that account to injure the British trade as much as any harbor in America."[7]

Privateers brought nearly 500 British ships into Connecticut ports during the war, with New London receiving most of these.[8] The need of someone to receive and dispose of prizes led Congress in April 1776 to appoint Shaw as "Prize Agent" for New London and vicinity. Shaw was to see that all prizes were tried by the proper admiralty court, and after they had been legally condemned, to sell them and make an equitable distribution of the proceeds. In addition, he was to make a quarterly statement to the Marine Committee showing the prizes received, the sales effected, and the distributions of the proceeds made.[9]

In addition to his duties as Continental prize agent, Shaw served as Connecticut's "Naval Agent for the Colony." Appointed in July 1776 by the Connecticut Council of Safety, his duties included handling all naval supplies, and the care of such sick seamen as were sent into the port. Later, in October 1778, the Council of Safety appointed Shaw to the position of Marine Agent, which authorized him to equip all state vessels, direct their cruises, and receive and sell their prizes. His imposing stone mansion in New London became Connecticut's Naval Office.[10]

The military importance of New London harbor made immediate provisions for its defense a major consideration. In April 1775, the Connecticut Assembly appointed Gurdon Saltonstall, John Deshon and Thomas Mumford of New London to examine points of defense, and report on the best means of fortifying the harbor. They reported that three positions, Mamacock, Winthrop's Neck, and Groton Heights should be fortified, and that fourteen new cannon be secured.[11]

Because Mamacock and Groton Heights later become the sites of the most important harbor forts, Trumbull and Griswold, respectively, they warrant further description. The neck of land bounding New London harbor on the south, then generally known by its Indian name of Mamacock, presented a broad, irregular platform of rocks, rising twenty feet above the water, and connected with the mainland on the west by meadows and marshes. This rock point, which jutted out into the harbor, was a good site for a water battery. The most desirable site, though not as close to the ship wharves, was Groton Heights. Nearly opposite the commercial center of the harbor, the Heights offered a 120 foot commanding eminence, with a fairly level summit, less than 200 yards from the water's edge. Cannon placed there would command all of Groton and New London.

Although the New London Committee submitted its report to the governor and the Council of Safety, no immediate action was taken. A brief, though frightening, British foray on the town in July 1775 reemphasized the need for prompt action. On July 26, the British ships of war *Rose, Swan* and *Kingfisher* anchored in the lower harbor. The next day a small landing party spiked three cannon in the old battery near the lighthouse, some three miles from town.[12] Finally, on November 2, 1775, responding to the pleas of the New London Committee, Governor Jonathan Trumbull sent Colonel Jedediah Elderkin of the Council of Safety to view the harbor and report what fortification was necessary. On November 15, Colonel Elderkin sent back a report which concurred with the New London Committee's findings, and as a result the governor and Council of Safety, on November 22, issued orders for the work to commence. This was to be done under the direction of a local committee: Colonel Gurdon Saltonstall, Ebenezer Ledyard, John Deshon, Nathaniel Shaw, Parke Avery, and Josiah Waters.[13]

Once work was authorized, the main problem encountered was securing enough heavy cannon for the fortification. Few serviceable guns were available in the harbor, and the Iron Works at Salisbury, Connecticut could provide a few guns, but only if orders were submitted long in advance. Most of the heavy ordnance was finally secured, however, through the capture of over 100 cannon by Commodore Esek Hopkins in his New Providence (Bahamas) raid of March 3-4, 1776. This expedition, which was outfitted in New London, set sail from that harbor on February 17, and was the first major operation for the new Continental Navy. Two mariners from New London, Dudley Saltonstall and Elisha Hinman, commanded the ships *Alfred* and *Cabot*, respectively, two of the eight vessels in the expedition. On the expedition's return to New London in April 1776, thirty-four cannon were left to be distributed in the harbor's defenses. Nathaniel Shaw, in his report to Governor Trumbull, wrote:

> Sir: Inclosed is an Invoice of the wt. And Size of Thirty four Cannon Rec'd from Admiral Hopkins, Ten of which is landed at Groton, viz: 3-24 pdrs, 2-18 pdrs and 5-12 pdrs. The remainder [8-24 pdrs, 2-18 pdrs, 10-9 pdrs] are at New London and are moastly fitted on carriages.... The Nine pounders are but ordinary Guns, the others are all very good.[14]

Once ordnance difficulties were resolved, tools, building materials and labor had to be secured. This was not an easy task, and the progress of fort construction was delayed by the peculiar bureaucratic difficulties encountered, difficulties graphically illustrated by Francis M. Caulkins in her *History of New London*:

> In the case of these small fortifications, the legislature must first discuss the matter and pass the resolves; the governor and council of safety must take it up; Colonel Saltonstall must be consulted; Mr. Shaw must be summoned to Hartford, to give advice... The works begin, stop, go on. The governor and council are at the trouble of directing just the number of sledges, hammers, shovels, etc., that are to be provided. Timber, teams, tools and other necessary materials are to be procured by Colonel Saltonstall for Winthrop's Neck; by Ebenezer Ledyard, for Groton; and Nathaniel Shaw, for Mamacock.[15]

More than a year elapsed following the Council of Safety's authorization before any of the works constructed could rank as fortifications. Although still incomplete, the works at Mamacock and Groton Heights were named Forts Trumbull and Griswold, after Governor Jonathan Trumbull and Deputy Governor Matthew Griswold.

Congress, recognizing the need for regular garrisons in the New London fortifications, authorized Governor Trumbull on June 24, 1776, "to raise three Companies of Troops on the Continental Establishment of Pay, Rations, and Disbursements, to be stationed at New London."[16] Acting on this authority, the

Connecticut Assembly passed a resolution, which in addition to the Congressional provisions, allowed an extra premium or bounty of twenty shillings to new recruits.[17] The companies raised were designated as Matross Companies, a title which referred specifically to their major duty—serving artillery pieces. These companies were raised for one year's service, and by the resolution of the Connecticut Assembly on February 15, 1777, were to consist of one captain, one captain-lieutenant, two lieutenants, one lieutenant fire-worker, three sergeants, three corporals, one drummer, one fifer, eight gunners, and thirty-three privates. Pay ranged from eight pounds a month for the captain, to forty-three shillings per month for a private. In addition, each private or noncommissioned officer who supplied his own firearm and accoutrements would receive a bonus of twenty-two shillings.[18]

The commander of the Matross Company stationed in Groton was Captain William Ledyard. Described as a man "of fine form and good education for the times," Ledyard pursued his military duties with a special zeal. This doubtless was due to the fact that he was a native of Groton, and the lives of his wife Anne and nine children might depend on his actions. From the beginning of the war he had been active in local military affairs, including membership in the town military committee and committee of correspondence.[19] In recognition of his abilities, the Connecticut Assembly, in March 1778, promoted Ledyard to the rank of major, with command of all fortifications in New London and Groton. At the same time, the number of Matross Companies authorized was reduced to two, of fifty men each, with Captain William Latham of Groton to command Ledyard's old company at Fort Griswold, and the Matross Company at Fort Trumbull to be commanded by Adam Shapley of New London.[20]

Ledyard's appointment made him responsible for the supervision of all military affairs in New London harbor, which proved to be a formidable task. His most pressing concern was to maintain a sufficient force to meet any possible British attack. In addition to the provocations provided by privateers sailing out of New London, the British would well be justified in making a quick raid just to destroy the stockpiles of foodstuffs and military supplies located in the wharves along the waterfront. On paper, Ledyard had a force of some 100 regulars. In addition, he could count on the town's defenses being augmented by local militia in time of emergency. In 1779, this meant that some 2,300 men were available in the district, including 1,111 in New London and 551 in Groton. These numbers, as impressive as they seem, did not reflect the real strength available at any given time.[21]

The most important element of the harbor's defenses was to be the two companies of regulars stationed at Forts Griswold and Trumbull. Ideally, these were to be of full strength, and composed of men skilled in the serving of artillery pieces. Militia were not trained in the handling of garrison cannon, so vital to the defense of the harbor—a fact reiterated by Ledyard in a letter to Governor Trumbull in December 1778:

> I find the more I am acquainted with the Duty of belonging to a Fortification the more is the necessity of having proper Soldiers to Garrison them...Your Excellency is fully acquainted that the Militia in general are but of little Service in Working of Cannon, the Fortifications at Groton have now upwards of Thirty Cannon mounted in them which will require a hundred good experienced Soldiers to serve them...I give it as my opinion that Fortifications are of but very little consequence if they are to be defended by unexperienced Troops...[22]

Ledyard had great difficulties in recruiting men for the two Matross Companies, and their actual strength rarely exceeded half the normal complement. The biggest deterrent to service was insufficient pay. Throughout the war Major Ledyard urged Governor Trumbull to get the Assembly to vote for higher wages and bounties. The following communication is typical:

> I would beg leave to inform your Excellency that there is not the least probability of Captains Shapley and Lathams filling up their Companies upon the encouragement offered by the Hon. General Assembly at their last Session and I am informed that the Officers have concluded not to serve upon the encouragement then offered...the Security of the Fortifications

and harbor depends...in having men...and I have not been able to...pay the Soldiers that served in the Artillery Companies last year....[23]

The difficulties experienced in getting recruits in New London were just another example of a problem that plagued the American war effort. Men engaged in profitable commercial pursuits, and seamen awaiting another privateer cruise, were not going to enlist for love of country, especially when the pay (often in arrears) was in inflated state or Continental currency. Indeed, on some occasions Ledyard could not even feed his men. Such was the case briefly in January 1781, when he secured permission from the Council of Safety to "release said garrison on short parole, as he may think safe, leaving necessary guards" because they were "destitute of bread, etc."[24] Soldiers vital to the defense of the harbor were starving in the midst of plenty. Ledyard's feelings must have been similar to those of General George Washington at Valley Forge, who watched his men starve while merchants sold foodstuffs to the British in Philadelphia.

Major Ledyard was offered some encouragement in his efforts to maintain the security of the harbor by the quick response of the militia to alarms. Frequently during the war the British made forage raids on nearby Fisher's Island, and their naval vessels were constantly passing below the harbor while cruising on Long Island Sound. If intelligence advised of more hostile intentions, the militia was called up. The established signal for an alarm was the firing of two cannon from Fort Griswold.[25] An account of one such false alarm in August 1780 indicates how real the fear of British attack was:

Last Saturday an express arrived at his Excellency the Governor's from Fairfield, with an account of there being 150 sail of shipping collected at Huntington harbor which had 8,000 troops on board. As it was thought probable they might be destined to attack this post, a large body of militia were ordered into this town.[26]

Unfortunately, the frequency of alarms, which often disrupted the civilian pursuits of the militiamen, made them increasingly hesitant to turn out as the war progressed. When the British descended on New London on September 6, 1781, the alarm had been spread once too often with tragic results.

Although Ledyard had difficulties in getting recruits, he did manage to achieve considerable progress in the improvement of the harbor fortifications. Most of the effort was concentrated on Fort Griswold. In May 1777, the Connecticut Assembly appointed Colonel Samuel Mott to oversee and direct construction of the harbor forts, in the capacity of engineer.[27] He designed Fort Griswold, and supervised the initial construction. Work on the fort continued intermittently through 1781, but the works were largely complete by 1779. At the height of construction, in October 1778, Major Ledyard reported his progress in a letter to Governor Trumbull:

> With regard to Fort Griswold we have been raising the Parapets higher in order in part to give them a proper Slope which we have near compleated. We have also near compleated the Ditches both in widening and deepening them as well as Stoning up the inward part of the Ditches, hope soon to finish Pickiting the Fort.[28]

It is of particular importance to describe the appearance of Fort Griswold. Fortunately, several contemporary sketches and descriptions exist, and many other details of its construction can be gleaned from letters, such as the one above. The grass covered earth remains of the fort, which can be seen today in Groton, retain the basic outlines of the Revolutionary War fort, which was a rectangle, with bastions facing the river on the northwest and southwest corners. Stephen Hempstead of New London, one of the defenders of Fort Griswold on September 6, 1781, gave the following description:

> Its walls were of stone, and were ten or twelve feet high on the lower side, and surrounded by a ditch. On the wall were pickets, projecting over twelve feet; above this was a parapet with embrasures, and with a platform for the cannon, and a step to mount upon to shoot over the parapet with small arms. In the southwest bastion was the flagstaff, and in the side, near the opposite angle, was the gate; in front of which was a triangular breastwork to protect the gate....[29]

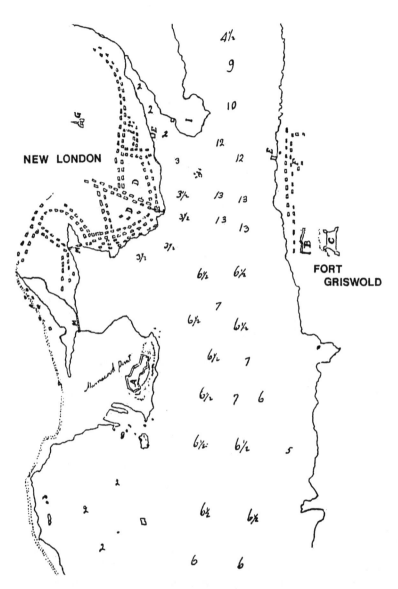

Samuel Mott map of New London Harbor, May 1776.

(National Archives)

16

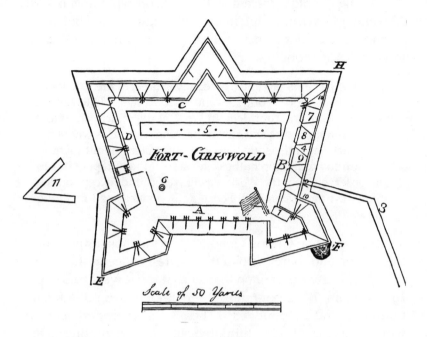

REFERENCES.

1. Magazine.
2. Salleè-Port.
3. a ditch leading to a Baty below.
4. Embrazine where Majr Montgomery fell.
5. Barracks.
6. Well.
7. 8. 9. Points where Ye Light comps. & Grenrs of ye 40th entered.
10. Guns yt much annoyed ye troops.
11. Ravlin that covered ye Gate.
F. a Rock not cut away which gives an entrance into ye work.
From E to F round the sides D, C & B ye work is fraiz'd.
on ye curtain A to the angle F it forms a barbette Batty.

H is at the southeast corner.
F is at the southwest corner.

During Arnold's descent on the town on September 6, 1781, Alexander Gray, an ensign in the 40th Regiment of Foot, made a simple sketch of the fort, including a key containing the following description:

The curtains [are] nearly forty yards each, the face looking to the Country, about Seventy Yards long. A Ditch about ten feet wide and four deep in Front of the [North and East] Faces, but there was no Ditch to the other two faces where the Rampart was sufficiently high without it, being about 16' from the ground to the top of the outer side of the Parapet...It is to be observed, that the Work was Frazed round, except on the Side next the Water, with Fence Rails pointed, and Inclining upwards.[30]

The works on Groton Heights were the most important in the harbor, and therefore had the greatest concentration of artillery. The array of cannon there was impressive, including 8-18 pounders, 17-12 pounders, 2-9 pounders, 1-6 pounder, 6-4 pounders, and 1-3 pounder.[31] These guns, if properly served, would make the British think twice before attempting to sail up river and bombard the town. Cannon, however, require gunpowder, and in addition to lacking the men to serve the pieces, Ledyard faced the problem of securing enough powder for muskets and cannon. Just how much he needed is indicated in a letter he wrote to Governor Trumbull in February 1779:

I find 58 Cannons at this Post [New London Harbor] from 4 to 18 pounders, these upon a medium will consume 4 pounds of Powder at one charge.... On an average about 20 Cartridges can be made from 1 pound of Powder allowing 60 Rounds to the Men in the Fort 1 1/2 Tons of Powder is necessary for the Musquet Cartridges, and about 4 or 5 Tons for the Cannon.[32]

Most of the powder came from France, although occasionally some was sent from the powder mill at Windham, Connecticut. Major Ledyard never received more than a few hundred pounds at a time, and was held strictly accountable for its use, as the following statement indicates:

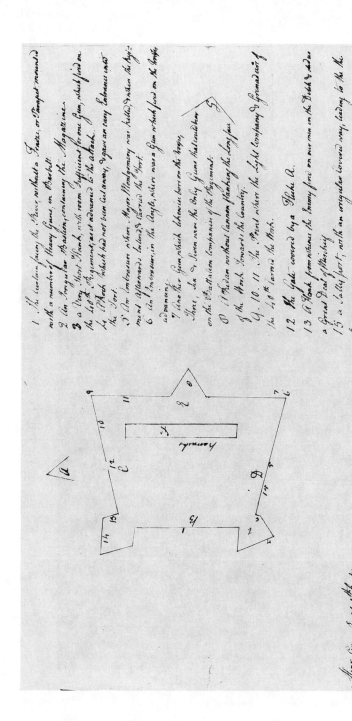

Ensign Alexander Gray's sketch of Fort Griswold, 1781.

View of Fort Griswold in 1904.

(Fort Griswold St. Park)

View of River Battery in 1904.

(Fort Griswold St. Park)

Voted: That Col. Ledyard receive from the powder-mill at Windham two barrels of musket powder for the use of the garrisons under his command. And Col. Ledyard is directed to give orders and take care that any waste of cartridges be accounted for by every person guilty of the same.[33]

As a result, Ledyard could not afford to waste powder in firing blanks, a necessary training exercise, for he barely had enough on hand to repel a limited attack. This too would have a bearing on the tragedy of September 6, 1781.

In addition to the work done on Fort Griswold, another fort was constructed in New London. Major Ledyard had determined that Fort Trumbull, which was little more than a water battery, was indefensible on the sides facing land. It was commanded in the rear by a large height, known as Town Hill, from which the enemy could bombard the fort and the town at will. In a letter to Governor Trumbull in February 1779, he urged that a fort be constructed on Town Hill.[34] The Assembly quickly approved his request, and armed with their authorization, he began construction in March. Militia did most of the work, and, as usual, Ledyard confronted numerous delays in getting the work completed. His difficulties were outlined to the Connecticut Council of Safety by James Wadsworth, a Council member, in a letter dated April 23, 1779:

> The militia have been encouraged to exert themselves on the Works with a prospect of being dismissed as soon as the Fortifications were completed—it has had good effect and there is a prospect of their being completed by Monday or Tuesday next, except the Platforms, the Timbers for which is some of it felled and hewed—But the teams are so poor and destitute of Hay it cannot be Carted at Present....[35]

Town Hill Fort was largely complete by August 1779, and mounted 2-12 pounders, 3-9 pounders, and 4-6 pounders.[36] Built largely of earth and wood, it required constant maintenance. This was a problem with all the harbor forts, and Ledyard had neither the resources nor the men to do more than simple repairs. Because of this neglect, and a constant lack of men, the forts were never in a proper posture of defense. Lieutenant Richard Chapman voiced his concern in a letter to Ledyard in March 1780:

> Sir, it Makes mee uneasy when I Consider the Weak Situation of this Post. I think it necessary for the safety of the State to have field Officers one on each side the River two Copenies of artilery or Metrosses with officers consisting of 60 Men Each One Company at Fort Trumbull the Other at Town Hill...The Reason which I give for two Companies is in Case of an atack to have two Officers with the Fieldpieces and a proper number of officers in Each Fort...I could wish some method would bee taken to Finish the Forts and to Put this Post in the Best Posture of Defence....[37]

Ledyard sent this report to Governor Trumbull as part of a memorandum concerning the state of the defenses, to which he added his own brief note of concern:

> ...as I am very anxious, considering the weak state we are in at this time, hope everything necessary will be ordered its safety as the fortifications want considerable repairing. Wish men might be got upon the ground in season for that purpose.[38]

The problems here outlined only begin to illustrate how inadequate the state of the defenses were to meet a British raid, which had been a distinct threat from the beginning of the war. The stage was set, and only the prompter was necessary for the beginning of the September 6 tragedy.

THE BURNING OF
NEW LONDON

A civilian walking along the waterfront in New London during late August 1781 might have been hard pressed to find visible signs of the hardships occasioned by six long years of war. Three new privateers were fitting out, and the captains were having little difficulty signing on crews of "Gentlemen Seamen and Landsmen, desirous of serving their Country and adding to their fortunes." Numerous prizes had been brought in during the last two months, and an interested reader would have found the following announcement in the *Connecticut Gazette* for August 31:

> To be sold at Vendue at New London on Thursday the 6th of September next, the fast sailing Prize Sloop *Hibernia*. Now lying at Edward Hallam's Wharf—about 70 tons Burthen, mounts 10 Carriage Guns, fit for a Privateer or Letter of Marque, also, a Number of 3 and 4 pound Cannon.[1]

The most important recent event was the arrival of the prize ship *Hannah*. On July 31, Captain Dudley Saltonstall, in the brigantine *Minerva*, captured this vessel, which proved to be the most valuable ship taken by a Connecticut privateer during the war. With its cargo of West Indian goods and gunpowder, appraised at about 80,000 pounds sterling, its capture caused great rejoicing among the merchants, and doubtless many of them treated the lucky crew to a round of flip or hot buttered rum at one of New London's many taverns.[2]

Not everyone in New London was concerned with the profits to be made from the sale of prize goods. A small number of merchants and farmers, lured by the prospects of British gold, engaged in illegal trade with the enemy. The feeding of the British army at New York, the supplying of the towns on Long Island, and the demand for manufactured articles in Connecticut, naturally made good markets. Whaleboats and other small craft slipped out of the harbor and adjoining inlets under cover of darkness to engage in this secret trade. In addition, many traders conveyed the latest intelligence on the state of affairs in the harbor to the British.[3]

Ledyard, now holding the rank of lieutenant colonel, was aware of the situation, and had been authorized to maintain several armed boats for patrol duty. But, as usual, he lacked the resources necessary to maintain a proper vigilance, as the following communication indicates:

> The illicit trade is of late carried on very briskly for want of men in our garrisons has prevented our keeping out our Boats. One of our Boats from Fort Trumbull last fryday cam athwart a Boat at Plumb Island, belonging to New London Great Neck, with a quantity of flour, two ferkins of Butter, sixty sythes, etc. which we took and brought off, the men made their Escape...[4]

Ledyard's difficulties were further complicated by the activities of those armed boat captains over whom he had no control. Many of these individuals, in addition to their cruising duties, had been authorized to "go on shore on Long Island to act against the enemy there." They abused their commissions, however, and "under colour and pretext thereof. . .unjustly and cruelly, plundered many of the friendly inhabitants there," and brought off their effects. As a result of numerous complaints, the governor and Council of Safety, on January 23, 1781, revoked all armed boat commissions. This act left Colonel Ledyard entirely to his own devices in attempting to stop illicit trade.[5]

Prior to the revocation of their commissions, the armed boat crews had conducted numerous raids across Long Island Sound against Loyalist strongholds. One of the largest of these havens for Loyalists was Fort Franklin, a stockade located on Lloyd's Neck, Long Island—nearly opposite the Sound from New London. From here organized groups of "loyal militia" conducted raids against the residents of the Connecticut coast. These militia were largely composed of men who desired to aid the King, but declined regular military service. Instead, they chose to fight in their own way, under a loose authorization that instructed them to plunder only "rebels" and allowed them to keep whatever they seized. Because so many of their attacks were launched under cover of night, the slogan "owls and ghosts and thieves and Tories" came to be closely associated among most residents of the Connecticut coastline.[6]

In practice, many of the raids were small scale—seizing sheep, poultry, cattle, corn—but that did not lessen the rising hatred between the two parties. In the words of Claude Halstead Van Tyne: "A natural result of this method of attack was to invite retaliation by the Whigs and to help evolve that hatred of the Tory which persisted long after the other wounds of the war were healed."[7]

The activities of the "Board of Associated Loyalists" (as they were called after 1780) at Fort Franklin were a major annoyance, and on two occasions sizeable raids were launched against it. On the evening of September 5, 1779, Major Benjamin Tallmadge led an expedition of 150 dismounted Light Dragoons against the stockade. In the attack he captured most of the garrison without suffering any casualties, but accomplished little else. Two years later, on July 12, 1781, a small force of American and French regulars attacked the fort, but were repulsed.[8]

There is some indication that Governor Trumbull had been planning to launch an expeditionary force against Fort Franklin from New London, but the British raid of September 6 abruptly halted the arrangements. At a meeting of the Council of Safety on August 22, 1781, he read a letter he had received from General Samuel H. Parsons, which described the defenses of

Lloyd's Neck in detail. Following this he discussed the possibilities of such an operation, and his proposals met with the approval of Thomas Mumford of Groton, who was in attendance. On September 8, 1781, Trumbull wrote to Mumford:

> The Project lately proposed in Council, when you was present, being, on this Occasion, in some Degree revived and brought under Consideration (to return the blow), I have to request you will at your Discretion, somehow with Secrecy discover and communicate Intelligence easily as may be; what suitable shipping may be probably engaged and employed for the Service at New London will not the Comanders of the three Brigantines, and other Armed Vessels be ready to attempt the Enterprise.[9]

At the time of the British raid, an impressive number of privateers were available in New London for Trumbull's proposed expedition, including the *Hancock* (18 guns, 100 men), *Mary Ann* (12 guns, 30 men), *Active* (10 guns, 60 men), and the *Gamecock* (4 guns, 30 men). After the British descended on the town, however, most of these vessels were in no condition to implement Trumbull's plan, as Mumford's reply to the governor on September 9 indicated:

> I can give your Excellency no encouragement from our privateers, the Two Brig't I am concerned in are sunk/ to save them/ their Sails and Riggin all consumed in Stores, one other has no guns, so that only one remains fit for duty, unequal to the plan proposed.[10]

Although the British commander-in-chief, Sir Henry Clinton, had considered raiding New London before, the demands of the campaign farther south had always held a higher priority. In early September 1781, however, conditions changed when Clinton received intelligence that Franco-American naval and land forces were heading for the Chesapeake, clearly indicating an attack on the army of Lord Cornwallis in Virginia. Forced to abandon his preparations for an attack on Newport, Clinton decided to hold his army in New York, but as he "was unwilling that the preparations for that service should be wholly lost, without some attempt being made to annoy the enemy's coasts and some endeavor to cause a diversion some-where," he issued marching orders for the attack on September 2.[11]

Clinton's decision was as much out of a desire to satisfy the demands of his vocal subordinate Benedict Arnold as it was out of any recognition that a military diversion was needed. Arnold had been earnestly seeking an independent command since his defection to the British in September 1780. Egged on by a desire to assert his new loyalties and prove his military merit, the "Dark Eagle" criticized Sir Henry's inactivity. As early as December 1780 he had volunteered to lead two warships into New London harbor to capture a 500-ton prize vessel, and in subsequent months he urged raids on either New London, Providence, or Boston.[12] His frustrations were outlined by a friend, William Smith, in his diary on August 25:

> I visited Arnold. He is greatly disconcerted. None of his propositions of Service are listened to, and he despairs of any-thing great or small from Sir H. Clinton, whom he suspects at prolonging the War for his own Interest. He wants me to sig-nify Home his Impatience, his Ideas, and his Overtures....[13]

Clinton could not have chosen a com-mander more familiar with his objective, for Arnold, a native of Nor-wich, Connecticut, had many former friends and acquaintances in New London, including Nathaniel Shaw. Con-trary to the belief of many Americans at the time, there is no evidence that Arnold accepted his as-signment for reasons of personal vengeance. Ap-parently, he viewed his

Benedict Arnold.

new command simply as an opportunity to prove his military skills, and was determined to execute the mission with all his customary zeal.

Although there has been some speculation that Clinton planned to conduct more than a limited raid, his marching orders clearly refute that notion. The troops were to take blankets, kettles, canteens, and two days' provisions, but were not allowed horses or tents. Clinton's ultimate objectives were to cut out or destroy the *Hannah* and other prize vessels, destroy the large cache of naval and other stores located in New London, and to effect the release of dozens of British naval prisoners known to be held there.[14] By the evening of September 2, preparations were underway, and the troops embarked on September 4. Two British officers stationed in New York, Lieutenant Frederick Mackenzie of the 23rd Regiment of Foot (The Royal Welsh Fusiliers), and Captain John Peebles of the 42nd Regiment of Foot (The Black Watch) both recorded in their diaries some of the details of Arnold's expedition:

> September 1: An Expedition is immediately to go against New London under the command of Arnold, to destroy some shipping, and a quantity of Stores there. It is a remarkable place for Privateers. (Mackenzie)
> September 2: A number of the Small vessels belonging to the Quarter Master General's Department went thro' Hellgate early this Morning, to Whitestone, where they are to receive the troops going with General Arnold. (Mackenzie)
> September 2: An Expedition going on Under Arnold supposed against Connecticut.
> The 40th. 54th. & 38th. Regts., Robinson & Buskirks Provincial Corps all assemble at Newtown this day, & Embark tomorrow at Whitestone...(Peebles)
> September 3: The Amphion and Recovery went safe thro' Hellgate at 10 this Morning. Those ships, with the vessels already in the Sound, are to Convoy Arnold's Expedition. (Mackenzie)
> September 4: The Expedition under Arnold sailed this Morning from Whitestone at 5 oClock, with a fair wind. (Mackenzie)[15]

Arnold's force of 1732 men and officers was transported by 24 vessels, including the warships *Amphion, Recovery, Beaumont,* and *Lively*. The bulk of the force was composed of three regular British "Regiments of Foot"—the 38th, 40th, and 54th, and a detachment of Hessian Yagers. The rest of the force was composed of Loyalist units—Arnold's own "American Legion," the 3rd Battalion of the New Jersey Volunteers, and the Loyal Americans.[16] In addition to those troops that embarked from New York, about 120 men, under the command of Colonel Joshua Upham, joined him at sea. These were part of the Loyalist Refugee Corps stationed at Lloyd's Neck, and were composed largely of the armed boat crews who had harassed the Connecticut coast so many times before.[17]

Clinton made sure to provide a nucleus of veterans, both regular and loyalist. The 40th Regiment of Foot had seen action at Fort Washington, fought at Princeton, participated at the Brandywine, and held the Chew House at Germantown, the defense of which figured prominently in the American defeat. Most recently much of the regiment had been stationed in the Caribbean, with a tour of duty as marines aboard Admiral Sir Samuel Hood's fleet.[18] The 54th took part in the expedition against Charleston in 1776, fought in the Battle of Brooklyn in August of that year, and participated in the defense of Rhode Island against the attack of the French fleet under Count D'Estaing during July and August of 1778. Perhaps most significantly, the 54th had participated in Governor William Tryon's raid on the Connecticut coastal towns of New Haven, Fairfield, and Norwalk in July 1779.[19] The 3rd Battalion of the New Jersey Volunteers, largely composed of men of Dutch descent from Bergen County, had seen action with Clinton in all his major campaigns since 1778, and had received numerous citations for unit discipline and performance. In the words of Adrian Leiby: "At a time when all too many Tory refugees were content to sit...drinking their ale and complaining of the government, Sir Henry was understandably delighted with his Bergen County Dutch Loyalist troops...who made up a larger number of his provincial soldiers than many a whole colony had supplied, and...acted like veterans.[20]

Arnold's transports arrived off the harbor about one o'clock on the morning of September 6, but due to a sudden shift of wind to the north, were unable to anchor until about 9:00 A.M. This more than eight-hour delay destroyed the element of surprise for which Arnold had hoped. Sergeant Rufus Avery, who was on sentry duty at Fort Griswold that evening, spotted the fleet about three o'clock, and reported his sighting to Captain William Latham, the fort commander. Latham in turn informed Colonel Ledyard. When Ledyard arrived, he immediately sent off express riders to spread the alarm to the militia companies, and ordered alarm guns to be fired from the fort. Sergeant Avery, who fired one of the cannon, wrote:

> Capt. William Latham took charge of one gun that was discharged at the northeast part of the fort, and I took charge of the gun on the west side of the fort, so as to give a "larum" to the country.... We discharged the regular "larum." Two guns was the regular "larum," but the enemy understood that, and they discharged a third gun similar to ours and timed it alike, which broke our alarm, which discouraged our troops coming to our assistance.[21]

The effect of Ledyard's alarm guns was largely eliminated by the British firing of a third cannon. This was a clever stunt, for it was well known that three guns was the signal given when a prize ship arrived—quite a different warning than a hostile fleet! This three-gun signal had been so often heard in the surrounding countryside that it caused little stir among the militia, whose subsequent tardiness in arriving had disastrous results. Avery Downer, a resident of Preston and an assistant surgeon for the 8th Regiment of Connecticut Militia, later recalled its effect: "I well remember the morning of the alarm two guns from the fort in a given time was the alarm. This the enemy well understood, and they fired a third, by which we in Preston were deceived, being fourteen miles distant."[22]

The sighting of Arnold's fleet near the Lighthouse (some three miles from town) caused mixed reactions among the townspeople. Many supposed that it was just another plundering party, after livestock on nearby Plumb Island. Others, including the privateer captains, decided to assume the worst, as Arnold's report indicated:

> As soon as the Enemy were alarmed in the Morning, we could perceive they were busily employed in bending sails, and endeavoring to get their Privateers and other ships up Norwich River [Thames], out of our reach, but the wind being small, and the tide against them, they were obliged to anchor again.[23]

Colonel Ledyard had no doubts about their intentions, as the result of a little known piece of intelligence he received the day before. Captain David Gray, a spy for Washington who had come into the confidence of General Clinton as an "agent," rode into Fort Griswold on the evening of September 5 and informed Ledyard that "arnol [sic] lay in huntington harbor with a number off men and no dout if the wind Should Bee fair he would visit newlonnon Before morning the next morning."[24] Ledyard had known Gray since 1778, when that agent had informed him of the activities of British spies in the region.

In the seven hours between the sighting of the fleet and the first landing of British troops about 10:00 A.M., hectic preparations were underway to meet the expected attack. Ledyard had decided to concentrate his efforts on a defense of Fort Griswold, and did all in his power to gather recruits. He did not have much to work with, and all the inadequacies heretofore mentioned were painfully clear to him. The regular garrisons of Griswold and Trumbull combined could muster some fifty men.[25] He concentrated his efforts on getting local militia, and seamen from the privateers, into the fort to augment his defenses. Privateersmen were of particular value, for many were trained gunners who could have served the cannon in the fort. Neither would respond in any numbers, and by 9:00 A.M. Ledyard had only about 140 men at Griswold.

Ledyard's inability to get volunteers was not surprising. In the case of the militia, he had to contend with their fear of being trapped in a closed work, with no avenue of escape. With the seamen, however, his requests were simply ignored, as they chose to look out for their own safety or that of their vessels.

Lacking men to impress recruits, he even resorted to the desperate measure of firing on some of the privateers as they fled up river, but to no avail. Several of New London's prominent citizens, in a letter to the new commandant of the harbor in April 1782, cited reasons for Ledyard's difficulties:

> ...if the late worthy Col. Ledyard had only fifty good men in the Fort under his absolute command, he with them might have empressed and compelled into its defense two or three hundred seamen and others.... But instead of this he was as a man without hands, and could get none into the fort only by persuasion. He gave out his positive orders for all seamen to repair over to the Fort.... But he was neglected with impunity. He was disobeyed because the laws are not adequate for the punishment of disobedience of orders....[26]

In addition to his futile attempts to secure recruits, Ledyard had to make up for the lack of powder and supplies by quick "requisitions." The powder needed by his garrison was available in abundance in New London, but was part of the Continental stores. Acting on Ledyard's authority, Guy Richards, Commissary at New London, sent over 900 pounds of powder to Fort Griswold. This task was carried out by John Holt, a ship joiner and storekeeper for Captain John Deshon. When Holt arrived at Fort Griswold, he stayed with the garrison, and was killed in the assault that afternoon. Other supplies were also sent, including twenty-four barrels of beef, "well pak'd and pickled."[27]

At about ten o'clock Arnold's troops landed in two divisions of about 800 men each, one on each side of the harbor. On the Groton side, where Arnold believed he would meet the stiffest resistance, he sent his best soldiers—the 40th and 54th Regiments of Foot, half of the Hessian Yagers, and the 3rd Battalion of the New Jersey Volunteers. The Groton Division was placed under the command of Lieutenant Colonel Edmund Eyre, who was also regimental commander of the 54th. The New London Division, under Arnold's direct command, contained the 38th Regiment of Foot, Colonel Upham's Refugees, the American Legion, the Loyal Americans, and the rest of the Yagers.[28]

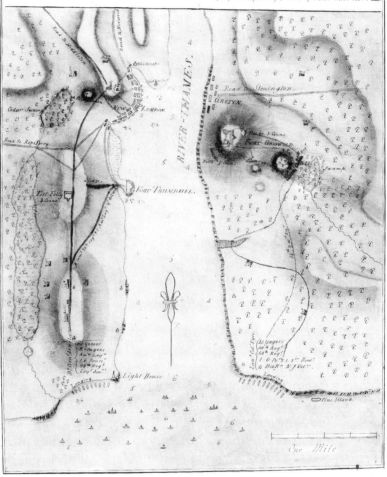

Captain Daniel Lyman map of New London Harbor, 1781.

The British met no resistance to their landing on the Groton side, but in New London, it was a different matter. A mixed force of civilians, militia, and privateersmen drifted down to Brown's farm, near the Lighthouse, to fire at the soldiers as they put into boats to come ashore. This group, though small, had some distinguished members, including Captain Seth Harding (late captain of the Continental frigate *Confederacy*), Captain Charles Bulkely (commanding the sloop *Active*, then in the harbor) and Captain John Deshon. Their bullets were met by a cannonade from the armed vessels *Association* and *Colonel Martin*, belonging to Colonel Upham's command, which Arnold had delegated to cover the landing. One of the sharp-shooters, John Hempstead, wrote:

> I got there Sometime Before they landed and there was But About forty men arm'd. Wee watted while the enemy was maning there botes. After they were all mand they Opend there brode Sides upon Both Shores, and all landed under ther Cannon whos balls flew over Our heads like hale Stones untill they ware all landed.[29]

Arnold prudently chose to land his Yagers first, who quickly spread out, took cover, and secured the beach. About 120 of these green coated Hessians accompanied the expedition, and unlike the rest of the troops, carried rifles. These soldiers were expert marksmen, and were generally used in flanking parties or as advanced guards. Using American "frontier" tactics, they exchanged shots with Hempsted and the others, who, being few in numbers and afraid of being trapped, quickly fell back. As they did so, the rest of the British landed, formed in columns, and advanced at the slow march.

The British columns, with Colonel Upham's Refugees and sixty Yagers in advance, proceeded up the Town Hill Road (now Ocean Avenue) to New London Center, a march of about three miles. They were met along the way by sporadic musket fire from the militia, but nothing as effective as that which the British had faced on their retreat from Concord in 1775. In fact, the militia were notoriously inaccurate, and during the whole afternoon the British only suffered twenty-two casualties, eight of these being men captured.[30] The lack of an organized defense was due to the absence of a central command, and the undisciplined nature of the "soldiers" themselves. One observer, fifteen year old Jonathan Brooks, captured the confusion as the would-be defenders sought a course of action:

> At the head of the road we fell in with about one hundred citizens, volunteer soldiers armed and equipped. My father dismounted and joined them. The party then fell into conversation about how they should manage, having no commanding officer. Some who had no experience in war matters were for fighting at any odds...but Captain Nathaniel Saltonstall, who once commanded the ship Putnam, said..."I will not be such a fool as to stand here open breasted and be shot down by the very first volley of the enemy's fire."[31]

While the group was talking with Saltonstall, Colonel Joseph Harris, commander of the Independent Militia Companies in New London, rode up. On his appearance the group took heart at the possibility of some kind of leadership. Instead, the Colonel informed them that, "You must excuse me gentlemen, as I have a violent sick-headache this morning, and can hardly sit my horse." With that, he rode off, and the group, following Saltonstall's suggestion that "each man take care of himself, and get a shot at the enemy as best he can," dispersed. So much for organized leadership in New London![32]

About eleven o'clock the main British column came within half a mile of Fort Trumbull. At this point General Arnold detached four companies of the 38th Foot, under Captain Millet, to attack the fort. Millet was joined by a company of the American Legion commanded by Captain Nathan Frink, a Loyalist from Pomfret, Connecticut. Frink, an aide to General Arnold, was assigned as a guide to the column, for he was well familiar with the town. Had he come under less trying circumstances, he might have spent a pleasant visit with his sister Lucy, who was then residing in New London.[33]

Millet's column met only token resistance from the men at Fort Trumbull. The fort had not been designed to deal with a rear assault, and in that quarter, only 3-6 pounder guns were mounted.[34] In any event, little could be expected from Captain Adam Shapley with a command of only twenty-three men.

Captain Shapley charged his pieces with grape shot, and after firing a single volley at the enemy's approach, spiked them and took his command to Fort Griswold. During this brief skirmish the British suffered five casualties, and Shapley had a man wounded by musket fire as his command crossed the river.[35]

Concurrent with Millet's assault on Fort Trumbull was Arnold's own attack against Town Hill Fort. At the time of the attack, the fort mounted 6-12 pounders, which if properly manned could effectively cover both the rear of Fort Trumbull and the main roads into the town. When Arnold approached, however, only a few militia and townspeople were gathered inside. Their fire, though brisk, was hindered by the presence of their own militia between the enemy and the fort. John Hempsted was near the fort at this time, and later recalled that, "When the forts opened upon the Enemy the Shot fell Short, and wee ware between two fires." Hempsted continued his retreat, even taking the time to help a friend hide a case of "holland jinn" in a nearby patch of weeds. The rest of the defenders fled, but one remained in the vicinity long enough to yell out, "Wilkom God damyou to fort NonSence" as the British entered the fort.[36]

While Arnold directed the attack on "Fort Nonsense," Colonel Upham's command proceeded to move against Post Hill, on the northern edge of town. The unhindered flight of some of the American ships disturbed Arnold, who hoped that artillery fire from this hill would sufficiently cripple them to enable his soldiers to reach and destroy them. His plan of coordinating the efforts of army and navy in destroying the shipping was foiled by the early alarm, as the report of Captain John Bazely, commander of the frigate *Amphion* (and commodore of the fleet) indicated:

> The armed vessels and boats I immediately afterwards ordered to be put in preparation under the direction of Captain Shepherd of the Recovery, to proceed up the River and act in conjunction with the army, at any moment their assistance was required to and in effecting the destruction of the port of New London. . .which would have finally taken place, but for the alarm guns. . .by this means I was deprived of getting hold of

their shipping at anchor in the stream, which. . .proceeded. . .up the river so far as to prevent by any possible means my taking or destroying of them.[37]

Colonel Upham captured the hill about noon, suffering two casualties in the process. Here his command endured a heavier fire, as his report discloses: "This height being the outpost was left to us and the Yagers. Here we remained, exposed to a constant fire from the rebels on the neighboring hills, and from the fort on the Groton side, until the last was carried by the British troops."[38] Once situated on the hill, the Colonel directed the fire of a six pounder brought with the column against those ships still in range. This effort, along with the fire from the captured guns at Fort Trumbull, did not succeed, for the wind came up again and the tide changed, thus enabling the vessels to escape upriver.

The entrance of Arnold's men created a scene of great confusion. Civilians who had not responded to the early alarm now made desperate attempts to gather their valuables and exit as quickly as possible. Jonathan Brooks was caught in their midst:

> ...when I came to the head of the cove the street was so crowded with the fleeing women and children, all loaded with something, that I had to move slowly. They inquired where the enemy were. I said "they will be among you within five minutes if you delay." Their loading was soon thrown down, and they started on a quick pace.[39]

Some individuals, however, took advantage of the chaos to plunder the public stores. The warehouses along Water Street, which contained the cargo of the *Hannah*, were looted. As young Jonathan Brooks stood by his home, waiting for the arrival of the Redcoats, five or six "shabby looking fellows" passed by shouting "by God, we'll have fine plunder by and by." Soon after this he heard a great noise from the direction of the warehouses, and upon mounting a nearby fence to get a look at the cause of the commotion, noticed some "thirty or forty people were loading themselves with plunder and scamping [sic] off."[40]

Americans were responsible for most of the plundering of private property. This was evident to the first historian of the tragedy, Francis Caulkins, who wrote: "It was afterward well understood that most of the spoil and havoc in private houses was the work of a few worthless vagrants of the town, who prowled in the wake of the invaders, hoping in the general confusion not to be detected."[41] Because of the great destruction wrought by the raid, however, it suited the purposes of American propaganda to charge these crimes on the British. On September 13, the Norwich Packet claimed that, "some houses were plundered; the soldiery seemed to be under no regularity, and everyone was at liberty to commit what devastation he thought proper."[42]

Arnold expressly forbade his soldiers to plunder private property or to molest the inhabitants. For the most part these orders were obeyed, but the provocation provided by sharpshooters from the houses triggered some incidents of wanton destruction. On Manwaring's Hill, where the British had been harassed by sharpshooters and the fire of a small fieldpiece, the detachment that captured the position ransacked the nearby home of Robert Manwaring, and set fire to it. Fortunately for the owner, the fire was extinguished by a passerby before any real damage could be done. On other occasions, the Yagers, operating independently of supervision, succumbed to temptation and stuffed their packs with "necessaries." On September 14 the Connecticut Gazette advertised the contents of the pack of one Hessian who had the misfortune to be captured:

> Found in a prisoner's pack, taken the 6th instant, 3 small pieces Holland, a small piece of scarlet broadcloth, a common prayer book, a checked linnen handkerchief, a comb and a pair of scissors. In the same pack were sundry articles of plate and jewelry, for which owners have appeared. Also found...an American Ensign.[43]

With the town secure, Arnold could direct his efforts to destroying all property of military value—the real objective of the raid. In order to accomplish this most effectively, he organized several torch parties, and took care to see that each had at least a few members familiar with the community. He had little difficulty in arranging this, for many Connecticut Loyalists were with the expedition. One of these was Daniel Lyman, a native of New Haven and a Yale graduate, who had served as a local magistrate until the outbreak of the war, when his loyalties forced him to leave his home. His family, like so many others, was divided by the conflict—his sister was the wife of Peter Colt, Assistant Commissary General for the state of Connecticut.[44]

The torch of destruction was first lighted at the north end of town. During the assault on Post Hill, a flanking party from Upham's column set fire to the house of Captain Picket Lattimer, who commanded one of the Independent Militia Companies from New London. If we can believe John Hempsted, the fact that Lattimer's house was the first to be burned is rather ironic in light of the following:

> I maid my way to quaker hill, and there I found I should say 5 hunderd men, sum arm'd and sum no armes. Whild I was there majer Darrow Came Riding Down, and Said to the men why the Devel don't yoo Go down and meet the Enemy? Picket Latimer sd as he was there that he would not Resk his life to Save other mens property, tho he was Capt. Of the Endependent Company att that time.[45]

The destruction of Lattimer's home was soon followed by the burning of the town mill and printing office on the northern edge of Winthrop's Cove. From here the British went on to Winthrop's Neck, where they systematically destroyed all the property there save one private residence. Leaving the Neck, the torch parties moved south along present day Main Street, laying waste to several private residences and outbuildings, the most valuable being that of General Gurdon Saltonstall, who lost his house, two stores, a shop and a barn.[46]

Whereas the sparks were kindled on the northern end of town, the real inferno began with the destruction along Water and Bank Streets, where the most important shops and warehouses were located. On Water Street, Arnold personally supervised the incendiary activity, which proved to be the most devastating of all. Here ten or twelve vessels were burned at their moorings, one of which contained a large quantity of gunpowder, unknown to Arnold. The results he outlined in his report: "The explosion of the powder, and change of wind soon after the stores were fired, communicated the flames to part of the town, which was, notwithstanding every effort to prevent in, unfortunately destroyed."[47]

Arnold's claim that the firing of part of the town was accidental was not accepted by the townspeople, who looked upon the event as another example of his perfidy. The Norwich Packet captured the sentiments of the time:

> There is the greatest absurdity in this part of the narration; for in many instances where houses were situated a great distance from any stores, and contained nothing but household furniture, they were set on fire, notwithstanding the earnest cries and intreaties of the women and children in them; who were threatened with being burnt up in their houses if they did not instantly leave them.[48]

The Packet account clearly goes to extremes, for there is no evidence to show that Arnold personally condoned wanton destruction, or that he viewed the burnings with the apparent satisfaction of a Nero. Contrary to contemporary propaganda, several incidents support Caulkins' contention that, on the whole, Arnold's orders were given "with some reference to humanity and the laws of civilized warfare."[49] Where the residents remained behind to protect their dwellings, they were generally treated well. Such was the case with Molly Colt, daughter of Captain Nathaniel Colt, whose pleas on behalf of her sick father saved the house. Similar pleas by the daughter of Commissary Guy Richards saved his home.[50] On Bradley Street, eight or ten houses were spared because the guide informed the head of the column that, "In this street there are no shops, no stores—it is the Widow's Row."[51]

Arnold's own conduct gives evidence that he tried to supervise the destruction as closely as possible, and did not authorize the burning of any buildings out of personal vengeance. He proceeded with the advance party that reached the north end of town, and from a vantage point near the First Burial Ground, observed the course of the devastation.[52] As the efforts shifted to the town center, he changed his location, using the opportunity to direct that certain houses be spared. One of these was the home of Captain Elisha Hinman, a celebrated privateersman who was a friend of Arnold's before the war. While in the vicinity of the Hinman house, Arnold may have had his closest brush with death. According to a widely circulated local tradition, Mrs. Abigail Hinman's indignation over Arnold's treason outweighed her gratitude, and while viewing the scenes of destruction around her, she became so angry at him that she seized a gun, aimed it and pulled the trigger, but it misfired. This incident prompted 19th century Arnold biographer Isaac Arnold to write: "The Lord did not on that day deliver Sisera into the hands of this modern Jael."[53]

The destruction in New London was largely completed by mid-afternoon, and it was extensive. In the center of town, the market wharf, old magazine and battery, courthouse, jail, Episcopal church, and several neighboring shops were all destroyed.[54] South of town the devastation was just as complete—all the boats and fishing craft, and several houses and shops, were destroyed along Long Bridge Cove.[55] Several prominent merchants suffered heavy losses, including Edward Hallam, Joseph Packwood, and Nathaniel Shaw. Shaw's own stone mansion was set afire, but the blaze was extinguished by a neighbor before much damage was done.[56] Not even the homes of reputed loyalists were spared, for such an act might have caused patriot reprisals. According to legend, Arnold ate dinner at the home of James Tilley, a Loyalist living on Bank Street, but even before they rose from the table the building was in flames over them.[57] In all, 143 buildings were consumed by the flames, including 65 houses, 37 stores, 18 shops, 20 barns, and 9 public and other structures. Some 97 families were left homeless.[58]

The British left New London about four o'clock. Throughout their stay they had been harassed by musket fire, but the Americans would not interfere with their activities due to lack of numbers. As the British pulled out, they pursued them, encouraged by the prospect of a fleeing enemy. Eight prisoners were taken, mostly Hessians, who were probably stragglers. During the afternoon the Americans lost four killed, and ten or twelve wounded.[59]

THE BATTLE OF
GROTON HEIGHTS

As heart-rending as the scenes of destruction were in New London, they paled before the horrible carnage that occurred on Groton Heights. Lieutenant Colonel Edmund Eyre's columns got underway about ten o'clock, and pressing into service a local boy, who had been found herding cattle, as a guide, they followed the cart path to the fort.[1] Rough terrain hindered their progress, but they were not met by any resistance along the route, a fact due to a crucial decision made by Colonel William Ledyard at a council of war held earlier that morning. In discussing possible strategies with his officers, Ledyard asserted his belief that the fort should be held, and wanted all efforts directed to convincing the militia companies to join the garrison. Captain Amos Stanton, a Continental Army officer home on leave, and a volunteer, maintained that such a defense would be impractical, because it was already evident that the militia were not going to consent to serve in a closed work from which they could not escape. Instead, Stanton suggested meeting the British at the beach, harassing them from behind cover, and slowly falling back. Using these tactics Ledyard could be guaranteed the services of most of the present militia, and at the same time could convey a false impression of American strength. The British would be forced to proceed cautiously, buying time for outlying militia companies to arrive in overwhelming numbers. Stanton's suggestion apparently did not gain support among the other officers, and Ledyard decided to stick to his original plan. He may have been influenced by promises of immediate help, but this is not certain.[2]

In retrospect, Ledyard's decision was a mistake. Major weaknesses in the fort's defenses were plainly evident, including the rotting of the gun platforms, the caving in of sections of the ditch, and breaks in the completed sections of the abatis (felled trees, stripped of leaves, with sharpened branches) adjoining the ditch. More grievous, however, was the lack of prepared ammunition for the cannon. Without "fixed cartridges" of powder with which to load each piece before the shot, loading would have to be done by dipping ladles into a keg of powder and measuring out the proper charge. A time consuming procedure, this could be quite dangerous in the heat of battle, when unprotected powder could be set off by flying sparks. With trained gunners this task was risky enough, but most of the men who would serve the cannon this day were inexperienced.[3]

Captain Adam Shapley's company arrived from Fort Trumbull about 11:30 A.M., increasing the garrison to some 165 officers and men.[4] Stephen Hempstead, Shapley's first sergeant, recalled years later that they "were received by the garrison with enthusiasm, being considered experienced artillerists, whom they much needed."[5] The shortage of gunners was a real concern for Ledyard, who had twenty-two cannon within the main fort, each requiring a minimum of four men to serve them. Other than his regulars, he could only count on the services of a few veteran mariners, experienced in handling cannon. One of these was Captain Elias Halsey, a refugee from Long Island who had seen service in the French and Indian War. Another, Captain Peter Richards, abandoned his ship, the privateer *Hancock*, on Ledyard's call, and joined with several of his crew.

Unfortunately, most of the garrison were either local militia or volunteers, with little or no combat experience. Many were young: Daniel Williams, a volunteer from Saybrook, was only fifteen, Captain Latham's son, William, Jr., fourteen, Stephen

44

Whittlesey, of Shapley's Matross Company, just sixteen. Many men were related: twelve bore the last name of Avery, nine of Perkins, five of Chester, five of Stanton, and five of Eldridge. Colonel William Ledyard was joined by two nephews, Youngs Ledyard and William Seymour, and his orderly Jordon Freeman, a free black. Another black, Lambo Latham, insisted on fighting by the side of his master, Captain William Latham. Even a Pequot Indian, Tom Wansuc, was present. There is great irony in the fact that he chose to risk his life for his neighbors near the very ground where his ancestors had been killed by Connecticut soldiers during the "Pequot War" in 1637.

Eyre's columns took over two hours to reach the vicinity of Fort Griswold, a distance of some three miles from their landing site. They had to proceed ahead of their artillery, which, under the supervision of Lieutenant Colonel Abraham Van Buskirk and the New Jersey Volunteers, did not reach the scene until after the battle. General Arnold, unaware of the difficulties being experienced across the river, soon became impressed with the necessity of seizing Fort Griswold, and ordered an immediate attack, as his report indicates:

> On taking possession of Fort Trumbull, I found the Enemy's ships would escape unless we could possess ourselves of Fort Griswold: I therefore dispatched an Officer to Lt. Col. Eyre with the intelligence I had received, and requested him to make an attack on the Fort as soon as possible; at which time I expected the Howitzer was up and would have been made use of.[6]

Just before noon the British got into position. Colonel Eyre formed the 54th Regiment behind a ledge of rocks about a half mile southeast of the fort, and Major Montgomery formed the 40th in the rear of a hillock, a short distance away.[7] Once organized, Eyre dispatched Captain George Beckwith with a flag to summon the surrender of the garrison. He approached to within two hundred yards of the fort when challenged by a musket shot and ordered to halt. Ledyard sent Capt. Elijah Avery, Capt. Amos Stanton, and Capt. John Williams to meet the flag, and hear the British terms. Sergeant Rufus Avery described the proceedings:

They immediately met the British flag, and received a demand to give up the fort to them. Our flag soon returned with the summons which was to surrender the fort to them. Inquiry was made of the council as to what must be done, and the answer was sent to the British flag that the fort would not be given up. Their flag went back to Col. Eyre's division, and soon returned to within about seventy rods of the fort, when they were again met by our flag, which brought back to Colonel Ledyard the demand if they had to take the fort by storm they should put martial law in force.[8]

The threat of martial law, which meant in essence that the survivors of the attack could expect no quarter, did not deter Colonel Ledyard. He ended the parley with the reply, "We will not give up the fort, let the consequences be what they may," and when Beckwith received the answer, he signaled the attack to commence.[9] The passing of flags occasioned a delay of almost an hour. Had Colonel Eyre decided to wait any longer, the whole tragedy might have been averted, for at the last moment Arnold decided to cancel the attack:

> On my gaining a height of ground in the rear of New London, from which I had a good prospect of Fort Griswold, I found it much more formidable than I expected, or than I had formed an Idea of from the information I had before received...I immediately dispatched a boat with an officer to Lt. Col. Eyre to countermand my first order to Attack the fort, but the Officer arrived a few minutes too late.[10]

Colonel Eyre disposed his columns so that the light infantry and grenadier companies of the 40th and 54th Regiments would assault the northeastern corner of the fort, under his direct command. This position was particularly difficult because of the ditch and a cannon that could enfilade the assailants from the northwest bastion. The light infantry and grenadiers were the finest men of both regiments, and it was common procedure to set them apart in order to tackle such an assignment. At the same time, Major Montgomery would lead the combined battalion companies of both regiments against the south and southwest flanks of the fort. In making this arrangement, Eyre was taking full advantage of the defensive weaknesses of Griswold, for only three cannon could bear directly on any assailants.[11]

As the British proceeded up the hill, they ran across their first obstacle—a small redoubt located about 300 yards east of the fort. Here they were met by a few rounds from the three pounder fieldpiece situated there, but upon their immediate approach, the few defenders fled. One of these men, Captain Elijah Bailey, could not get back to Fort Griswold as directed, and hid himself in a nearby cornfield. Captain Bailey lived on to the ripe old age of ninety, serving as postmaster of Groton for his last forty years. He died in August 1848.[12]

The British approached the redoubt in solid column, and as soon as they entered it, Captain Elias Halsey opened fire with an eighteen pounder situated on the eastern rampart of the fort. His first shot inflicted some twenty casualties, and forced the British to scatter.[13] Both groups of assailants dispersed, trailed their arms, and attacked at a quick step. Two or three times, however, they were driven back by a deadly fire of case shot and musketry from the fort, with heavy casualties. Colonel Eyre was critically wounded in the first assault, and Major Montgomery, regathering the bloodied men, seriously considered a withdrawal.

At this point, about a half hour into the battle, there was a general cease fire all along the line. Ledyard had suffered few casualties, and saw no reason to expend valuable ammunition until the British came close to the fort. He had made the best possible use of his motley garrison, particularly in the placement of his matrossmen and privateersmen on the cannon facing the direction of the assault. While Ledyard remained at the northern end of the parade ground, Captains Shapley and Latham directed the defense at the key southwest bastion. From here all the way to the southeast corner was a distinguished assemblage, including Captain Peter Richards and several of his crewmen, Lieutenant Richard Chapman, Sergeant Rufus Avery, and Sergeant Stephen Hempstead. Latham, Avery, and Hempstead bear particular mention because they provided the most informative accounts of the events in statements after the battle.[14]

During this lull in the fighting, a stray shot severed the American ensign from its halyards on the flagpole in the southwest bastion. Although it was instantly remounted on a pike pole, the British took the action to mean that the fort had struck her colors.[15] Encouraged by the apparent surrender, the soldiers rushed forward again, only to be met by a heavy fire as they approached the ditch. This time, however, they were not to be denied. Arnold described what happened:

> The troops approached on three sides of the work, which was a Square with flanks, and made a lodgement in the ditch, and under a heavy fire which they kept up on the works, effected a second lodgement on the fraizing, which was attended with great difficulty, as only a few pickets could be forced out, or broke, in a place, and was so high that the Soldiers could not ascend without assisting each other.[16]

Once in the ditch, the most furious fighting took place. Because of the height of the walls, the only way to get onto the parapet was with scaling ladders or by mounting the fraizing and then attempting to climb in through one of the embrasures. According to Captain John Peebles, "notwithstanding the difficultys & obstructions they met with, the want of Scaling ladders or any preparations for an Attack of that kind, & a brisk fire kept up from the work, they persver'd in their endeavors to get in." Led by the Major himself, Montgomery's columns finally managed to get a few men through the embrasures. As he entered, he was killed with a fifteen foot spear by Jordon Freeman. Several others were killed in a similar fashion, but the overwhelming strength and persistence of the British were too much, and the defenders were soon overpowered.[17]

On the northern side of the fort, the grenadiers and light infantry broke in about the same time. Rufus Avery described the action: "As soon as the enemy got round the fort one man attempted to open the gate. He lost his life. There was hard fighting some time before the second man made the trial to open the gate, which he did. Our little number...were soon overpowered."[18]

With the gate forced open and British soldiers pouring in from both sides, Colonel Ledyard determined that further re-

Two views showing a reconstructed battery at Fort Ligonier.
Similar features were faced by the British at Fort Griswold.

sistance was futile, and he ordered his men to lay down their arms. Because of the noise and confusion, many men did not comply, and their resistance continued. What happened next was described by Captain William Latham:

> ...After they had Opened the Gates and took Possession the Garrison was ordered to Cease firing, when he saw Col. Ledyard walking the Parade (to Appearance) Unhurt, and as soon as the Orders for to Cease Fire was known to be Genuine he answered them on the South of the Fort where was his station, at which time Col. Ledyard turned and walked towards the North Gate to meet the officer that Lead in the Troops, when he (the Deponent) set out to follow him, but before he got to him, the Col. was killed.[19]

Following the colonel's death, in the words of Sergeant Hempstead: "Then they wantonly went to shoting and Bayoneting of us tho quarters was continuously cryed for from Everyone but to no purpose."[20] Many of the British soldiers, infuriated by the loss of their comrades and by the supposed American surrender, began the indiscriminate slaughter of anyone at hand. Most of the victims were those members of the garrison who had obeyed Ledyard's orders to surrender. The fault was not entirely that of the British, however. Ensign Alexander Gray, who was with the 40th as they entered the works, made it clear that, "After the troops carried the work the Enemy fired from their Barracks and wounded several men."[21]

The horrible carnage that followed was graphically illustrated by the accounts of some of the survivors. Daniel Eldridge, a volunteer, later recalled:

> I was in the Fort at Groton when it was Taken by the Brittish Troops in Sept., 1781, and after the Enemy took possession of the Fort and our people Laid Down their arms, we perceiving by the conduct of the Enemy, that they gave no Quarter, but Insult and Savage Cruelty were Murdering all they come at, myself and a number of others sought for shelter in the Entrance of the Magazine, But they pursued us and fired in upon us where some of us were killed, the People of the Fort all the Time begging for Quarters.[22]

Some of the garrison, seeing the fate of their comrades, determined to sell their lives as dearly as possible. Captain Youngs Ledyard, on witnessing the death of his uncle, rushed into combat to avenge the act, and was killed.[23] Captain Amos Stanton did likewise and suffered the same fate.[24] Private Charles Chester, witnessing the murder of his two brothers, retained his musket and remained defiantly on the ramparts. He dispatched one British soldier who came at him with a bayonet, and would have fought to the death had not a British officer offered him quarter.[25]

Private Chester was one of several men who were spared as the result of desperate efforts by some British officers to stop the slaughter. One of these was Captain George Beckwith, who was one of the first officers to enter the works.[26] Like Major Pitcairn at Lexington six years before, Captain Beckwith had to try to restrain men who were at a fever pitch of rage. His attempts to establish order may have been further complicated by the fact that some of the men in the Battalion companies of the 40th were new recruits, inexperienced in combat and poorly disciplined. In light of subsequent charges by the Americans of British atrocity, these circumstances and the following statement by General William Heath must be considered:

> It is not meant to exculpate or to aggravate the conduct of the enemy on this occasion—but two things are to be remembered: first, that in almost all cases the slaughter does but begin when the vanquished give way;...Secondly, in all attacks by assault, the assailants...have their minds worked up almost to a point of fury and madness. . .and that consequently when a place is carried, and the assailed submit, the assailants cannot simultaneously curb their fury to reason, and in this interval many are slain in a way which cool bystanders would call wanton and barbarous, and even the perpetrators themselves, when their rage subsided would condemn....[27]

Finally, about two o'clock, it was all over. Captain Stephen Bromfield, who was now in command, entered the fort and ordered the signal for a cease-fire—the drumbeat.[28] He had good reason to fear for the lives of his own men, for many of the soldiers had been firing at those Americans who took cover

Section, North and East Walls

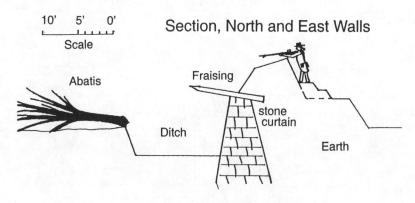

10' 5' 0'
Scale

Abatis

Fraising

Ditch

stone curtain

Earth

Section, South Wall

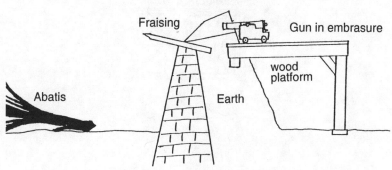

Fraising

Gun in embrasure

Abatis

Earth

wood platform

Section, West Wall

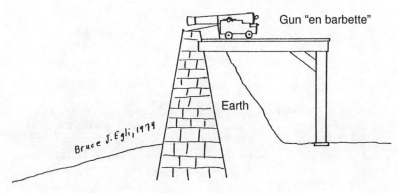

Gun "en barbette"

Earth

Bruce J. Egli, 1974

Main Gate (conjectural)

10'   5'   0'

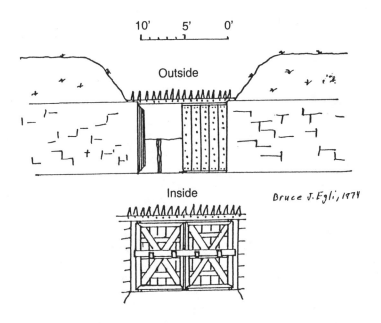

Outside

Inside   Bruce J. Egli, 1974

Barracks (conjectural)

10 yd.   5 yd.   0 yd.

Frame construction

View from Fort Griswold looking Southeast. The Battalion Companies of the 40th Regiment of Foot attacked across this ground. (Fort Griswold State Park)

at the entrance to the powder magazine, thus threatening to blow up the whole fort. The battle lasted only about forty minutes, with all but three of the American dead being caused after their surrender. The garrison suffered an immediate loss of 83 dead and 36 wounded, several of whom died within a few hours.[29] The British lost 48 killed and 135 wounded, or about one fourth of the men engaged.[30]

With the fort secure, Captain Bromfield directed his efforts to caring for his wounded and burying his dead. Those Americans still unhurt were ordered to assist, and all the doors from the Barracks were removed to serve as stretchers. The British dead, including Major Montgomery, were buried in the ditch of the ravelin that covered the gate.[31]

During this interval many of the less humane British soldiers stripped the prisoners of their personal effects.[32] Others were more kind, particularly toward the wounded who had been left to languish in the hot sun. Edward Stanton, who was bleeding profusely from an exposed wound in the breast, owed his life to Lieutenant Jacob Van Buskirk (son of the Colonel), who stanched the flow of blood using his own linen nightcap. This same officer offered him water, as he did to several other men.[33] Captain Beckwith directed a surgeon to dress the wounds of William Seymour, with whom he had made previous acquaintance in New York while Seymour was negotiating a prisoner exchange.[34]

At this point the British made hasty arrangements to leave. Captain Bromfield ordered the fort cannon spiked and had powder fuses set to the barracks and the powder magazine. At the same time he sent a detachment into Groton, where several buildings were burned.[35] Because he planned to blow up the fort, all the American wounded had to be quickly evacuated. It was during this evacuation that an accident occurred which formed a fitting anticlimax to the tragedy of the afternoon. Eight of the wounded who could not walk were loaded in the fort's ammunition wagon and taken down a steep hill to the waterfront. About halfway down the chain being used to stay the wheels broke, and the detachment escorting the wagon, fearing for their safety, let it go. It rolled the remaining 200 feet and crashed into a large apple tree stump at the foot of the hill. In the words of Stephen Hempstead, who was in the wagon: "the Seane was dreadful which none can describe but those unfortunate men that felt it we all lived to Reach the foot of the hill."[36]

The British quickly ran to the wagon, then saw to it that the wounded were deposited in the nearby house of Ensign Ebenezer Avery. The rest of the wounded were paroled on the condition that they not take up arms again until exchanged. To guarantee their good behavior, Ebenezer Ledyard, brother of the slain colonel, volunteered to go to New York as a hostage.[37] Another parolee, fourteen year old William Latham, Jr., was allowed to stay behind with his father on the condition that he promise "not to grow up to be a damned rebel."[38] The rest of the survivors were paraded to the waterfront, where they were loaded aboard two nearby sloops to be carried to New York. In their haste to leave, the British did not remain behind to see if the fuses lit would explode the powder, and as a result the fort was saved by the vigilance of a militia officer. Little damage was done to Fort Griswold other than the dismounting and spiking of the cannon.[39]

With the British on board their ships, the townspeople were able to emerge and lend a hand to the wounded. Two large hospitals were set up at the homes of Ensign Avery and James Bailey, where the wounded were attended by Dr. Joshua Downer and his son Avery, both of Preston.[40] Several of the men were in critical condition, including William Seymour, who had thirteen bayonet wounds, and Daniel Stanton, who had a leg wound and twenty-five cutlass gashes.[41] Sergeant Hempstead later captured the agony of the wounded that evening: "Such a night of distress and anguish was scarcely ever passed by mortal. Thirty-five of us were lying on the bare floor—stiff, mangled, and wounded in every manner, exhausted with pain, fatigue and loss of blood, without clothes or anything to cover us, trembling with cold and spasms of extreme anguish...."[42]

The scene at Fort Griswold was even more ghastly. The dead were still unburied, and many of the corpses, mangled or covered with dirt and blood, were barely recognizable. Twenty-three year old Anna Warner Bailey, whose husband Elijah had fought in the advanced earthwork, entered the fort at sunset to search for her uncle. She found him still alive, having been left for dead after fainting from a gunshot wound. Describing the scene, she was afterward recorded to have said: "If the earth had opened and poured forth blood instead of drinking in it, it could not have been more plentiful."[43]

Several others searched among the dead, including Mrs. Hempstead (who did not recognize her husband among the wounded), and Fanny Ledyard, Colonel Ledyard's niece. After viewing the corpse of her uncle, she returned to the wounded to lend whatever assistance possible. Sergeant Hempstead gratefully remembered her kindness years later: "Miss Fanny Ledyard, of Southold, L.I. (then on a visit to her uncle, our murdered commander)...held to my lips a cup of warm chocolate, and soon after returned with wine and other refreshments, which revived us a little. For these kindnesses she has never ceased to receive my most grateful thanks, and fervent prayers for her felicity."[44]

Arnold's fleet sailed from New London harbor about eight o'clock the next morning, and arrived in New York on September 9—its passage delayed by contrary winds.[45] General Clinton, though pleased with the destruction of the stores in New London, expressed concern over the heavy casualties. He wrote in his report:

> But whilst he draws the greatest satisfaction from the ardor of the troops which enabled them to carry by assault a work of such great strength as Fort Griswold is represented to be, he can not but lament with the deepest concern the heavy loss in officers and men sustained by the 40th and 54th regiments, who had the honor of the attack....[46]

Captain John Peebles was much more critical of Arnold's attack. The views expressed in his diary on September 9 may have reflected those of many others in Clinton's command: "Upon the whole this affair is judged to have been fool hardy in Mr. Arnold & throwing away mens lives to very little purpose."[47]

What Clinton had hoped to gain from the expedition is still unclear. The destruction of military stores in New London, though impressive, was hardly worth the cost in men and effort. Informed of Franco-American movements toward the Chesapeake on September 2, he may have hoped that Arnold's expedition would divert Washington's attention back north, away from Cornwallis. He had promised that officer such a diversion in a letter of September 2:

> By intelligence which I have this day received, it would seem that Mr. Washington is moving an army to the southward with an appearance of haste, and gives out that he expects the cooperation of a considerable French armament. Your Lordship, however, may be assured that, if this should be the case, I shall either endeavor to reinforce the army un-

der your command by all means within the compass of my power, or make every possible diversion in Your Lordship's favor.[48]

The raid, of course, did not divert Washington's attention. Clinton probably realized this would be the case, but ordered the expedition as a compromise from inactivity. He had compelling reasons for remaining inactive in New York, for he believed that the British retained naval superiority in the Chesapeake. As long as this was true, Lord Cornwallis was in no real danger. It was not until September 18 that Clinton learned of the results of the battle off the Chesapeake Capes, and by that time, it was too late to reinforce Cornwallis.[49]

The raid did nothing to enhance Arnold's reputation, and proved to be his last command against his former countrymen. He had to go to great lengths to prove that he had not condoned the wanton destruction of private property. Clinton exculpated him in his report:

> The commander-in-chief begs leave to express his obligations to Brigadier-General Arnold for his very spirited conduct on the occasion; and he assures that general officer that he took every precaution in his power to prevent the destruction of the town, which is a misfortune that gives him much concern.[50]

Nevertheless, as leader of the expedition, Arnold bore the ultimate responsibility for everything that occurred. He would have been better advised to have refused the command, for his presence in New London made him a more nefarious figure in the eyes of his former countrymen. Had the war continued any longer, the raid would have stirred the country to fiercer resistance. As it was, there were many people, who in light of the destruction and slaughter of that afternoon, considered the terms given Lord Cornwallis as erring grossly on the side of leniency.[51]

THE STRANGE DEATH OF
COLONEL WILLIAM LEDYARD

The incident most often recounted in narratives of the Battle of Fort Griswold is the alleged murder of Colonel Ledyard. According to popular accounts, the British officer in charge killed Ledyard with his own sword as he tendered it in surrender. The narrative of Sergeant Stephen Hempstead is typical:

> At this moment [of the garrison surrendering] the renegade Colonel commanding cried out "Who commands this garrison?" Colonel Ledyard, who was standing near me, answered: "I did Sir, but you do now," at the same time stepping forward, handing him his sword with the point towards himself. At this instant I perceived a soldier in the act of bayoneting me from behind. I turned suddenly round and grasped his bayonet, endeavouring to unship it, and knock off the thrust—but in vain. Having but one hand, he suceeding in forcing it into my right hip, above the joint, and just below the abdomen, and crushed me to the ground. The first person I saw afterwords was my brave commander, a corpse by my side, having been run through the body, with his own sword, by the savage renegado.[1]

Unfortunately, this account was written in 1826, when Hempstead was seventy-two years old, and was residing in St. Louis, Missouri. His own contemporary statements strongly

Stephen Hempstead, a sergeant at the fort.

suggest that he was not near the scene when the tragedy occurred, for in his sworn deposition before Samuel Mott in New London on April 11, 1782, he stated:

> When the garrison Saw the Barbarity of the Enemy and That they gave no Quarter, we having Laid Down our Arms and no way to Defend ourselves fled into the Barracks, and into the Entrance of the Magazine for shelter, But the Enemy pursued us (I being badly wounded in the arm) and being with those who fled into the Magazine, the Enemy Continued firing upon us while naked and unarmed, and followed up with their Bayonets, and I was run through with the bayonet....[2]

Hempstead had fled to the powder magazine for cover (after it became clear that the British were ignoring the "surrender") and received his bayonet wound in the hip there. This contradicts his later claim that he was wounded near the Colonel, and "crushed...to the ground," which would have placed him near the gate, the spot which is always cited as the place where Colonel Ledyard met his death.

Interestingly enough, Hempstead made no mention of the circumstances surrounding Ledyard's death in his contemporary written remarks about the battle. In a letter to Governor Trumbull on September 30, 1781, he stated only the following:

> They came on with Vigour and Resolution untill they had got under Cover of the walls of the Fort from our Cannons which made them of no use to us, we then repaired to our small Arms and lanses with a Resolution to repulse the enemy if possible which we maintained for some time when we had the misfortune to have the Hallards of our Colours shot away which the enemy thinking we had Struck to them, gave them Double Resolution in Scaling the walls which they affected but not without the loss of many men. Then they wantonly went to shoting and Bayoneting of us tho quarters was continually cryed for from Everyone but to no purpose....[3]

His deposition was equally as reticent:

> ...on the 6th Day of September, 1781, being a Sergeant in the Fort at New London, It being attacked by a party of Brittish Troops Commanded by General Arnold (The Traitor) and the Fort not being Tenable the Garrison Retreated Across the River to the Fort at Groton, where in a Short time we were attacked by another Large Party of Brittish Troops who after a short conflict carried the Fort by Storm, and after the Garrison surrendered The British Put to Death Col. Ledyard, our Commander, and a great number of other officers and soldiers of the Garrison, while they were begging for Quarter.[4]

On the basis of these accounts it is clear that Hempstead's 1826 narrative contains numerous embellishments. It is easy to imagine the aging veteran, already given to overstatement, putting himself at every point where the important events took place. That several of his statements are questionable is reflected in two other comments made concerning it. Dr. Avery Downer, of Preston, observed in 1851 that, "He published there [St. Louis] a narrative of the battle of Groton Heights—correct in some things and very incorrect in others."[5] On a more hu-

Interior of Fort from Southwest bastion, 1904. Spot where Col. Ledyard fell is enclosed by small fence.

(Fort Griswold St. Park)

morous note, Charles Allyn, of New London, while collecting material for a revised edition of *The Battle of Groton Heights* in 1881, received a brief letter concerning Hempstead's narrative. In the letter, the writer questioned Hempstead's ability to father a child fourteen months after the battle if he "lay eleven months as helpless as a child." The writer concluded: "Perhaps helpless did not mean akin so entirely paralyzed as it does to me."[6]

The only other frequently cited narrative by a member of the garrison which mentioned Colonel Ledyard's murder, was that of Sergeant Rufus Avery. Avery did not attest to witnessing the murder, nor did he mention the supposed dialogue that passed between Ledyard and the British officer. He wrote:

> Colonel William Ledyard was on the parade, marching towards the enemy under Capt. Bloomfield [Captain Stephen Bromfield] raising and lowering his sword.... I turned my eyes from Ledyard and stepped up to the door of the barrack, and saw the enemy discharging their guns through the windows. I turned myself immediately about, and the enemy had executed Col. Ledyard, in less time than one minute after I saw him.[7]

In a similar fashion the depositions of four other members of the garrison contained within the Trumbull Papers at the Connecticut State Library, do not mention the details of the incident. It is remarkable that these men (Lt. Obadiah Perkins, Solomon Perkins, Captain William Latham, and Daniel Eldridge) would neglect to mention so striking an atrocity.

A more positive clue to the probable fate of Colonel Ledyard is contained in an undated letter which Sgt. Avery sent to Governor Trumbull. In this he wrote:

> ...as I had so Great a Prospect of the Garrison, I took Particular Notis when the Enemy Came over the Paripit by the Gates first cleard the Platforme then Open'd the Gates then the Enemy Rusht in—Came ?, to one of our men he askt them for Quarters they dam'd him and put him to death, Likewise Colonel Ledyard fair'd his fait in the Same manner....[8]

Charles Eldridge, Jr., wounded near the powder magazine.

From Avery's letter, it appears that Colonel Ledyard was bayoneted, with several other men, while begging for quarter. This seems all the more probable in light of Hempstead's statement in his deposition that, "after the Garrison surrendered the British Put to Death Col. Ledyard, our Commander, and a great number of other officers and soldiers of the Garrison, while they were begging for Quarter."[9] Although no less brutal, Ledyard's demise in this fashion forms a pitiful contrast to a proud warrior slain while tendering his sword in an honorable capitulation!

Because none of the newspapers went into particulars on the death of Ledyard, the only contemporary evidence that he met his fate according to tradition is in a letter written by Thomas Mumford to Governor Trumbull on September 9, 1781. Mumford, who was not at the scene when it happened, wrote:

> ...Col. Ledyard finding the Enemy had gained possession of some part of the Fort and opened the Gate, having three men killed tho't proper to Surrender himself with the Garrison prisoners, and presented his Sword to an officer who Rec'd the same and immediately lunged in thro the Brave Commandant, when the Ruffians/ no doubt by order/ pierced him in many places with Bayonets.[10]

An interesting piece of physical evidence which challenges Mumford's statement is the vest Ledyard wore when he was killed. This item of clothing, made of striped linen, is located in storage at the Connecticut Historical Society. It was donated in 1841 by Mrs. Maria Ledyard, the widow of Col. Ledyard's youngest son, William Pitt Ledyard. Rather than showing evidence of being "pierced...in many places with Bayonets," the vest contains only two holes, one on each side, and about six inches from the arm. Both holes are near the seams of the front pieces of the garment, and do not go through the back (most peculiar for a man stabbed in front by his own sword). The width of the holes and the nature of the tears in the fabric could certainly have been made by a sword, but equally suggest that he might have been killed by a thrust from a triangular bladed bayonet, of the type carried by most British soldiers on their "Brown Bess" muskets.[11]

The picture of a valiant Colonel murdered while making an honorable surrender, and a helpless garrison put to the sword, made great propaganda for the Continental press. This was apparently how the incident was to be used when Governor Trumbull wrote the following letter to Thomas Mumford, of Groton, on September 8, 1781:

> Desire you will carefully collect and state those Transactions and all material circumstances, more especially the Treatment of Col. Ledyard, the unfortunate Garrison, procure the same to be authenticated and forwarded to Me, for Such Improvement as may be here after thought proper.[12]

As the years passed, the murder of Colonel Ledyard became an accepted fact. The many histories of the United States published in the nineteenth century included accounts that differed little from the following:

> Ledyard finally surrendered his sword to Major Bromfield, who instantly plunged it in the heart of the prisoner, and the bloody example was followed so mercilessly, that nearly every man of the garrison was butchered. The Groton Massacre is another horrible stain on the British arms, and was fitly perpetrated under the lead of Arnold.[13]

It was not until William Harris published *The Battle of Groton Heights* in 1870 that any real question of the validity of the incident appeared in print. Nevertheless, the story still stands. The traditional version remains in a more recent authoritative military history of the war, Christopher Ward's *War of the Revolution* (1952).[14]

Besides the death of Colonel Ledyard, the incident of British atrocity repeated most frequently was that of the wagonload of wounded that rolled uncontrolled down the hill as Fort Griswold was being evacuated. The wagon incident was not mentioned at all in the September 7 issue of the *Connecticut Gazette*, but a week later full details of the atrocity appeared:

> The following savage action committed by the troops who subdued Fort Griswold on Groton Hill, on thursday last, ought to be recorded to their eternal infamy. Soon after the surrendry of the fort, they loaded a wagon with our wounded men, by order of their officers, and set the waggon off from the top of the hill, which is long and very steep; the waggon went a considerable distance with great force, till it was suddenly stopped by a tree; the shock was so great to those faint and bleeding men, that part of them died instantly; the officers ordered their men to fire on the waggon while it was running.[15]

Several falsehoods are immediately apparent from the statement made by Sergeant Hempstead, one of the wounded. In a letter sent to Governor Trumbull, Hempstead wrote:

> The soldiers drew the waggon out of the Fort to the top of the hill when chain'd one of the fore wheels of the waggon with a small chain. . .they no sooner started the waggon than the chain broke and they let the waggon go amain down the hill which is very steep and they with the greater part of the Troops then Paraded on the hill a Huzzawing to see the seane but did not fire on us as been Reported.[16]

His account does not differ substantially from one written by Captain William Latham:

> The well and wounded was ordered to set down on the Ground together untill between 5 to 6 o'clock P.M., when all that Could Walk were ordered down the hill and a wagon loaded with others after which they Brought a pair of horses

and tried to geer them in the wagon but could not as the wagon was not fitted in the form of theirs. then the officers ordered a number of Soldiers to take it down the hill and Return with it Imediately for the Rest/ who took it to the brow of the hill where they all left it but three who chained one wheele and then moved the wagon. The hill being steep the whool [sic] left it, as Soon as it started the chain Broake, and the wagon Run about thirty Rods and brought up against a tree which shocked the people much....[17]

From these statements it is clear that the incident was accidental, and that everyone lived through the ordeal.

As time passed, the magnitude of the affair continued to grow. When the Connecticut Assembly, in January 1782, authorized Samuel Mott and Rufus Lathrop "to take and procure all the necessary Depositions for investigating a full knowledge of the Cruelties and Barbarities committed by the Enemy in their attack," those individuals took particular care to get statements concerning the event.[18] Obadiah Perkins stated that, "the Waggon was loaded with the Wounded and let run down the Hill about forty Rods."[19] In the same vein, Rufus Avery wrote that he saw "wounded Prisoners run Down the hill in the Cart then the Officers and Soldiers give a chere and hopt all the Prisoners should be skivered that Night."[20]

Years later, when the passions of the moment had cooled, Avery revised his narrative. He wrote:

> They loaded up our very large, heavy ammunition wagon that belonged to the fort with the wounded men who could not go themselves, and about twenty of the soldiers drew it out of the fort and brought it to the brow of the hill on which the fort stood, which was very steep, and about thirty rods distance. As soon as the enemy began to move the wagon down the hill, they began to put themselves in a position to hold it back with all their power. They found it too much for them to do; they released their hold on the wagon as quick as possible to prevent being run over by the wagon themselves, leaving it to run down the hill with great speed. It ran about twelve rods to a large apple tree stump, and both shafts of the wagon struck very hard, and hurt the wounded men very much.[21]

Unfortunately, his comrade in arms, Sergeant Stephen Hempstead, departed from the truth of his earlier account, and added numerous embellishments to his 1826 narrative. This account, often cited, has been accepted as the truth:

> Those that could stand were then paraded, and ordered to the landing, while those that could not, (of which number I was one) were put in our ammunition wagon, and taken to the brow of the hill (which is very steep, and at least 100 rods in descent) from whence it was permitted to run down by itself, but was arrested in its course, near the river, by an apple tree.... We remained in the wagon more than an hour, before our humane conquerors hunted us up, when we were again paraded and laid on the beach....[22]

Residents of Groton have not forgotten the tragedy of September 6, and many reminders of that fateful afternoon remain. The earthwork ruins of Fort Griswold, retaining the essential outline of the Revolutionary War fort, are now part of Fort Griswold State Park. Towering nearby is a 127 foot monument, dedicated on September 6, 1826.[23] Upon entering, visitors are solemnly reminded that, "Zebulon and Naphtali were a people that jeoparded their lives unto the death in the high places of the field."[24]

View of Fort Griswold and Groton Monument from rampart of River Battery, 1904.

APPENDIX

Arnold's Report, September 11, 1781[1]

1781
11th Sept.—
Brigadier General Arnold's letter to the Commander in Chief, giving an account of the Expedition to New London.

Sir—   Sound.—Off Plumb Island.   8th Sep.:81.
I have the honor to inform your Excellency, that the transports with the detachments of troops under my orders, anchored on the Long Island shore on the 5th Inst. At 2 oClock P.M., about 10 leagues from New London, and having made some necessary arrangements, weighed anchor at 7 o'Clock. P.M., and Stood for New London with a fair wind. At 1 o'Clock the next Morning we arrived off the harbour, when the wind suddenly shifted to the Northward, and it was 9 o'Clock before the transports could beat in. At 10 o'Clock the troops in two divisions, and in four debarkations were landed; one on each side the harbour about 3 miles from New London. That on the Groton side, consisting of the 40th and 54th Regiments, and the New Jersey Volunteers, with a Detachment of Jagers and Artillery, was under the Command of Lieut. Colonel Eyre. The Division on the New London side, consisted of the 38th Regiment, The Loyal Americans, The American Legion, Refugees and a Detachment of 60 Jagers; who were immediately put

in motion on their landing, and at 11 oClock being within half a mile of Fort Trumbull, which Commands New London harbour, I detached Captain Millet with 4 Companies of the 38th Regiment to attack the Fort, who was joined on his march by Capt. Frink with one Company of The American Legion. At the same time I advanced with the rest of the division West of Fort Trumbull, on the road to the town, to attack a Redoubt which had kept up a brisk fire upon us for some time, but which the Enemy evacuated on our approach. In this work we found 6 pieces of Cannon mounted and 2 dismounted. Soon after I had the pleasure to see Captn. Millet march into Fort Trumbull under a Shower of Grape shot, from a number of Cannon, which the Enemy had turned upon him; and I have the pleasure to inform your Excellency, that by the sudden attack and determined bravery of the troops the Fort was carried with the loss of only 4 or 5 men killed and wounded. Captain Millet had orders to leave one Company in Fort Trumbull, to detach one to the Fort we had taken, and to join me with the other two Companies. No time was lost on my part in gaining the town of New London. We were opposed by a small body of the Enemy with one field piece, who were so hard pressed, that they were obliged to leave the piece, which being Iron, was spiked and left.

As soon as the Enemy were alarmed in the Morning, we could perceive they were busily employed in bending sails, and endeavoring to get their Privateers and other ships up Norwich River, out of our reach, but the wind being small, and the tide against them, they were obliged to anchor again.

From information I received before and after my landing, I had reason to believe Fort Griswold, on Groton side, was very incomplete; and I was assured (by friends to Government) after my landing that there were only 20, or 30 men in the Fort, the Inhabitants in general being on board their ships and busy in saving their property. On taking possession of Fort Trumbull, I found the Enemy's ships would escape unless were could possess ourselves of Fort Griswold: I therefore dispatched an Officer to Lieut. Colo. Eyre with the intelligence I had received, & requested him to make an attack on the Fort as soon as possible; at which time I expected the Howitzer was up and would be made use of. On my gaining a height of ground in the rear of New London, from which I had a good prospect of Fort Griswold, I found it much more formidable than I expected, or than I had formed any Idea of from the information I had before received. I observed at the same time that the men who had escaped from Fort Trumbull, had crossed in boats and thrown themselves into Fort Griswold, and a favorable wind springing up about this time, the Enemy's ships were escaping up the River, notwithstanding the fire from Fort Trumbull and a Six pounder I had with me. I immediately dispatched a boat with an Officer to Lieut. Colo. Eyre to countermand my first order to Attack the fort, but the Officer arrived a few minutes too late. Lieut. Colo. Eyre had sent Capt. Beckwith with a flag of truce to demand the surrender of the fort, which was peremptorily refused, and the attack had commenced. After a most obstinate defence of near 40 minutes the Fort was carried by the superior bravery and perseverance of the Assailants. The attack was judicious and spirited, and reflects the highest honor on the Officers and troops, who seemed to vie with each other in being the first in danger. The troops approached on three sides of the work, which was a Square with flanks, and made a lodgement in the ditch, and, under a heavy fire which they kept up on the work, effected a second lodgement on the fraizing, which was attended with great difficulty, as only a few pickets could be forced out, or broke, in a place, and was so high that the Soldiers could not ascent without assisting each other. Here the coolness and bravery of the troops were very conspicuous, as the first who ascended the fraize, were obliged to Silence a 9 pounder which enfiladed the place on which they stood, until a sufficient body had collected to enter the work, which was done with fixed bayonets thro' the Embrazures, where they were opposed with great obstinacy by the Garrison with long spears. On this occasion I have to regret the loss of Major Montgomery, who was killed by a Spear in entering the Enemy's works: also of Ensign Whillock of the 40th, who was killed in the attack. Three other Officers of the same Regiment were wounded. Lieut. Colo. Eyre, and three other Officers of the 54th Regiment were also wounded, but I have the satisfaction to inform Your Excellency that they are all in a fair way to recover.

Lieut. Colo. Eyre, who behaved with great gallantry, having received his wound near the work, & Major Montgomery being killed soon after, the Command devolved on Major Bromfield, whose behavior on this occasion does him great honor.

Lieut. Colo. Buskirk with the New Jersey Volunteers and Artillery, being the 2ed debarkation, came up soon after the work was carried, having been retarded by the roughness of the Country. I am much obliged to this Gentleman for his exertions, altho' the Artillery did not arrive in time.

I have enclosed a return of the killed and wounded, by which Your Excellency will observe that our loss, tho' very considerable, is very short of the Enemy's, who lost most of their Officers, among whom was their Cammander Colonel Ledyard. 85 men were found dead in Fort Griswold, and 60 wounded, most of them mortally. Their loss on the opposite side must have been considerable but cannot be ascertained. I believe we have about Seventy prisoners, besides the wounded, who were left paroled. Ten or twelve of the Enemy's ships were burnt: among them three of four armed vessels, and one loaded with Naval Stores. An immense quantity of European and West India goods were found in the stores; among the former the Cargo of The Hannah, Captain Watson, from London, lately captured by the Enemy, the whole of which was burnt, with the stores, which proved to contain a large quantity of powder unknown to us. The explosion of the powder, and change of wind soon after the stores were fired, communicated the flames to part of the town, which was, notwithstanding every effort to prevent it, unfortunately destroyed.

Upwards of 50 pieces of Iron Cannon, were destroyed in the different works (exclusive of the guns of the ships) a particular return of which I cannot do myself the honor to transmit to your Excellency at this time.

A very considerable magazine of powder, and barracks to contain 300 men were found in Fort Griswold, which Captain

Le Moine of the Royal Artillery had my positive directions to destroy; an attempt was made by him but unfortunately failed: he had my orders to make a second attempt: the reason why it was not done, Captain Le Moine will have the honor to explain to Your Excellency.

I should be wanting in justice to the Gentlemen of the Navy, did I omit to acknowledge that upon this expedition, I have received every possible aid from them. Captain Bazeley has made every exertion to assist our operations; and not only gave up his Cabin to the sick and wounded Officers, but furnished them with every assistance and refreshment that his Ship afforded.

Lord Dalrymple will have the honor to deliver my dispatches. I beg leave to refer your Excellency to His Lordship for the particulars of our operations on the New London side. I feel myself under great obligations to him for his exertions.

Captain Beckwith who was extremely serviceable to me, returns with his Lordship. His spirited conduct in the attack of Fort Griswold does him great honor, being one of the first Officers who entered the works. I beg leave to refer your Excellency to him for the particulars of our operations on that side, and to say, I have the highest opinion of his abilities as an Officer.

I am greatly indebted to Capt. Stapleton (who acted as Major of brigade) for his spirited conduct and assistance, in particular on the attack of Fort-Trumbull, and his endeavors to prevent plundering, (when the publick stores were burnt) and the destruction of private buildings.

The Officers and troops in general behaved with the greatest intrepidity and firmness.

I have the honor to be &c. &c—
Bendt. Arnold

NOTES

Chapter I

1. Charles Oscar Paullin, *The Navy of the American Revolution: Its Administration, its Policy, and its Achievements* (Cleveland, OH: The Burrows Bros. Co., 1906), 362. The population of New London in 1774, including Montville and Waterford, was 5,888. For this and other information, see Timothy Dwight, *Travels in New England and New York*, 4 vols. (Cambridge, MA: Harvard University Press, 1969), 2:367-370.
2. John W. Barber, *Connecticut Historical Collections: Containing a General Collection of Interesting Facts, Traditions, Biographical Sketches, Anecdotes, etc. Relating to the History and Antiquities of Every Town in Connecticut, with Geographical Descriptions* (New Haven, CT: B. L. Hamlen, 1836), 289. One pound sterling was worth roughly fifty dollars in 1965. See Gerald W. Mullin, *Flight and Rebellion: Slave Resistance in Eighteenth Century Virginia* (New York: Oxford University Press, 1972), 6.
3. Major Patrick Ferguson, Map, May 1779, Sir Henry Clinton Papers, William L. Clements Library, University of Michigan, Ann Arbor. (Hereafter cited as Clinton papers.)
4. Ernest E. Rogers, *Connecticut's Naval Office at New London During the War of the American Revolution* (New London, CT: New London County Historical Society, 1933), 54.
5. Louis F. Middlebrook, *History of Maritime Connecticut During the American Revolution, 1775-1783*, 2 vols. (Salem, MA: The Essex Institute, 1925), 2:98-99. The first commander of the General Putnam was Thomas Allen, of New London, with a crew of 150 men. Constructed at Winthrop's Neck, the ship had an armament of 20-9 pounder cannon. All materials for her construction came from Connecticut; the total cost came to 50,000 pounds sterling. See Rogers, 54-55.
6. Albert E. VanDusen, *Connecticut* (New York: Random House, 1961), 157.
7. Middlebrook, 1:ix.
8. Van Dusen, 158. With the shifting of British land operations to the South in 1779, there was a marked increase in privateer activity. Fewer British naval vessels were available for patrol duty, and as a result, the years 1779-1780 saw the highest level of privateering in the war. In May 1779 alone, eighteen prizes were brought into New London.
9. Paullin, *The Navy of the American Revolution*, 93-95.
10. Rogers, *Connecticut's Naval Office*, 22. Like other states, Connecticut's legislators created a standing committee called the Council of Safety to deal with emergencies that might arise when the legislature was not in session. The Committee was headed by Governor Jonathan Trumbull and Deputy Governor Matthew Griswold, and had as members such prominent men as Eliphalet Dyer, Benjamin

Huntington, William Williams, Jedediah Elderkin, and Joshua West. The Council held most of its meetings at the "War Office" in Lebanon, adjacent to the home of Governor Trumbull.

11. Charles J. Hoadly, ed., *The Public Records of the Colony of Connecticut*, 15 vols. (Hartford: Case, Lockwood and Brainard Co., 1890), 14:434. (Hereafter cited as *Connecticut Colony Records*.)

12. *The Connecticut Gazette* and the *Universal Intelligencer*, July 28, 1775.

13. *Connecticut Colony Records*, 15:177, 181.

14. William Bell Clark, ed., *Naval Documents of the American Revolution*, 6 vols. (Washington, D.C.: Government Printing Office, 1964-1972), 4:1250-1251.

15. Francis Manwaring Caulkins, *History of New London, Connecticut* (New London: Published by the author, 1852), 517.

16. *Naval Documents of the American Revolution*, 5:713. In May 1776, Colonel Richard Gridley, Chief Engineer for the Continental Army, traveled to New London and completed a series of maps of the state of the harbor defenses which he transmitted to General Washington. See Paul K. Walker, *Engineers of Independence: A Documentary History of the Army Engineers in the American Revolution, 1775-1783* (Washington, D.C.: Government Printing Office, 1981), 74-76.

17. *Connecticut Colony Records*, 15:436.

18. Charles J. Hoadly, ed., *The Public Records of the State of Connecticut*, 4 vols. (Hartford: Case, Lockwood and Brainard Co., 1894-1942), 1:175. (Hereafter cited as *Connecticut State Records*.)

19. Dumas Malone, ed., *Dictionary of American Biography*, 22 vols. (New York: Charles Scribner's Sons, 1928-1944), 11:94.

20. *Connecticut State Records*, 1:514.

21. *Ibid.*, 2:385.

22. William Ledyard to Governor Trumbull, December 1, 1778, Trumbull Papers, Connecticut State Library, Hartford. (Hereafter cited as CSL.)

23. William Ledyard to Governor Trumbull, April 12, 1779, Trumbull Papers, CSL.

24. *Connecticut State Records*, 3:288.

25. A statement concerning this alarm system can be found in the narrative of Sgt. Rufus Avery, of Groton, in William W. Harris, *The Battle of Groton Heights: A Collection of Narratives, Official Reports, Records, etc. of the Storming of Fort Griswold, the Massacre of its Garrison, and the burning of New London by British Troops under the Command of Brig. Gen. Benedict Arnold, on the Sixth of Sept., 1781*, rev. Charles Allyn (New London, CT: Charles Allyn, 1882), 30.

26. *Connecticut Gazette*, August 4, 1780.

27. *Connecticut State Records*, 1:315.

28. William Ledyard to Governor Trumbull, October 7, 1778, Trumbull Papers, CSL.

29. Harris, *Groton Heights*, 48. See Figures 1, 2, and 3.

30. Ensign Alexander Gray, Sketch, Sir Henry Clinton Papers, Clements Library, University of Michigan, Ann Arbor. (Hereafter cited as HCP).

31. Frederick MacKenzie, *Diary of Frederick MacKenzie: Giving a daily narrative of his military services as an officer of the regiment of Royal Welsh Fusiliers during the years 1775-1781 in Massachusetts, Rhode Island, and New York*, 2 vols. (Cambridge: Harvard University Press, 1930), 2:628. The information on Fort Griswold's cannon as recorded in MacKenzie's Diary is taken from the report of J. Lemoine, Captain of Artillery with General Arnold's expedition that was written on board Betsey Sloop in New London Harbor a few hours after the attack of September 6th.

32. William Ledyard to Governor Trumbull, February 1779, Trumbull Papers, CSL.

33. *Connecticut State Records*, 3:128.

34. William Ledyard to Governor Trumbull, February 1779, Trumbull Papers, CSL.

35. James Wadsworth to Governor Trumbull, April 23, 1779, Trumbull Papers, CSL.
36. *Connecticut State Records*, 2:385.
37. Lieutenant Richard Chapman to Major Ledyard, March 11, 1780, Trumbull Papers, CSL.
38. Middlebrook, *History of Maritime Connecticut*, 1:163-164.

Chapter II

1. *Connecticut Gazette*, August 31, 1781. Two of the most frequented taverns in New London were those of Nathan Douglass, at the "Sign of the Golden Ball" opposite the Post Office, and Joseph Waterman, at the "Sign of the Red Lion" near the Court House.
2. Middlebrook, *History of Maritime Connecticut*, 2:163-164.
3. Paullin, *The Navy of the American Revolution*, 370.
4. William Ledyard to Governor Trumbull, June 11, 1781, Trumbull Papers, CSL. Major Ledyard was promoted to the rank of lieutenant colonel by the Connecticut Assembly in January 1780.
5. *Connecticut State Records*, 2:110; 3:292.
6. Claude Halstead Van Tyne, *The Loyalists in the American Revolution* (New York: The Macmillan Co., 1902), 174.
7. Van Tyne, 182.
8. Frederic G. Mather, *The Refugees of 1776 from Long Island to Connecticut* (Albany, New York: J. B. Lyon Co., 1913), pp. 232-233. Major Tallmadge is best known for his apprehension of John Andre and the subsequent uncovering of Benedict Arnold's treason. He served as head of Washington's secret service; after the war he became a successful businessman in his home town of Litchfield, Connecticut. The town of Tallmadge, Ohio is named after him.
9. Governor Trumbull to Thomas Mumford, September 8, 1781, Trumbull Papers, Connecticut Historical Society, Hartford. (Hereafter cited as CHS.)
10. Thomas Mumford to Governor Trumbull, September 9, 1781, Trumbull Papers, CSL.
11. Henry Clinton, *The American Rebellion: Sir Henry Clinton's Narrative of his Campaigns, 1775-1782*, ed. William B. Willcox (New Haven: Yale University Press, 1954), 330.
12. William Smith, *Historical Memoirs From 26 August 1778 to 12 November 1783 of William Smith: Historian of the Province of New York; Member of the Governor's Council, and Last Chief Justice of that Province Under the Crown; Chief Justice of Quebec*, ed. William H. W. Sabine (New York: Arno Press, 1971), 349.
13. Smith., 434.
14. Frederick MacKenzie, *Diary*, 2:611. See also Clinton, *American Rebellion*, 330. As to Clinton's objectives, Charles Burr Todd went as far as to claim the following: "[It would] be a convenient base for certain predatory excursions into New England, which it is probable Clinton had long meditated, but, most important of all, it was within a day's march of Lebanon, the quiet country town where dwelt Gov. Jonathan Trumbull—Washington's 'Brother Jonathan,' and which contained the little store and counting house, which had long been recognized as the real 'war office' of the Continental Government, and the chief source of supplies for its army; and no doubt the hope of disturbing 'Mr. Trumbull' in his operations, and of ravaging the rich agricultural region near him. . .was one of the motives of the expedition." Charles Burr Todd, "The Massacre at Fort Griswold," *Magazine of American History* 7 (September 1881):162.
15. MacKenzie, *Diary*, 2:610-613. See also John Peebles' *American War: The Diary of a Scottish Grenadier, 1776-1782*. Edited by Ira D. Gruber. (Mechanicsburg, PA: Stackpole Books, 1998), 469.

16. "State of various corps going on Benedict Arnold's Expedition against New London," August 15, 1781, Frederick MacKenzie Papers, Clements Library.

17. Harris, *Groton Heights*, 110.

18. Willard M. Wallace, *Traitorous Hero: The Life and Fortunes of Benedict Arnold* (New York: Harper & Bros., 1954), 279. See also Philip R. N. Katcher, *Encyclopedia of British, Provincial, and German Army Units, 1775-1783* (Harrisburg, PA: Stackpole Books, 1973), 51-52.

19. *September 6 and 7, 1931: Sesquicentennial of the Battle of Groton Heights and the Burning of New London, Connecticut*, ed. Ernest E. Rogers (New London: Fort Griswold and Groton Monument Commission, 1931), 97. See also Katcher, 60. For an excellent account of Tryon's raid, and the role of the 54th regiment, see Thomas J. Farnham, "'The Day the Enemy was in Town:' The British Raids on Connecticut, July 1779" in *Journal of The New Haven Colony Historical Society*, Volume 24, No. 2 (Summer 1976), 3-63.

20. Adrian C. Leiby, *The Revolutionary War in the Hackensack Valley: The Jersey Dutch and the Neutral Ground 1775-1783* (New Brunswick, NJ: Rutgers University Press, 1962), 135.

21. Harris, *Groton Heights*, 30.

22. *Ibid.*, 84.

23. Arnold's report to General Clinton, September 11, 1781, cited in MacKenzie, *Diary*, 2:624.

24. John Bakeless, *Turncoats, Traitors and Heroes* (Philadelphia: J. B. Lippincott Co., 1959), 247.

25. Colonel Ledyard to Governor Trumbull, July 3, 1781, Trumbull Papers, CSL. In this letter Ledyard wrote: "...Could wish a detachment of about 30 men for Fort Trumbull, and twenty for Fort Griswold; Capt. Shapley's Company now consists only of about 12 men, Capt. Latham's of 31 including officers..."

26. Harris, *Groton Heights*, 125.

27. *Connecticut State Records*, 4:115.

28. Arnold's Report, cited in MacKenzie, *Diary*, 2:623.

29. John Hempsted narrative, cited in Harris, *Groton Heights*, 62.

30. British casualty figures cited in MacKenzie, *Diary*, 2:627. The heaviest casualties were in Arnold's American Legion, with 1 killed, 6 wounded, and 2 listed as missing. In the Hessian Yager detachment, 2 were wounded and 5 listed as missing. The 38th Regiment of Foot reported 2 men wounded and 1 man missing.

31. Jonathan Brooks narrative, cited in Harris, *Groton Heights*, 76.

32. Harris, 76-77.

33. Lorenzo Sabine, *Biographical Sketches of Loyalists of the American Revolution*, 2 vols. (Port Washington, NY: Kennikat Press, Inc., 1966), 1:449. A British Regiment of Foot consisted of ten companies. During the New London raid, the 38th had a strength of 377 men, which meant that Millet had about 150 men at his disposal to attack Fort Trumbull.

34. According to the British Inventory of Ordnance destroyed on September 6, Fort Trumbull contained 12-18 pounders, and 3-6 pounders. See MacKenzie, *Diary*, 2:628. Shapley's difficulties were compounded by the poor condition of the existing works. In a letter to Governor Trumbull on September 19, 1781, Christopher Leffingwell, commander of a militia company from Norwich, wrote: "The platform in Fort Trumbull is Rotten...The Works there Very Extensive and cannot be completed without an amazing expence nor defended without a great many men..." Trumbull Papers, CSL.

35. MacKenzie, *Diary*, 2:624.

36. Harris, *Groton Heights*, 65.

37. French Chadwick, ed., *The Graves Papers and Other Documents Relating to the Naval Operations of the Yorktown Campaign July to October, 1781* (New York: Naval Historical Society, 1916), 108-109.
38. Col. Upham's report cited in Harris, *Groton Heights*,109.
39. Brooks narrative in Harris, *Groton Heights*, 79.
40. Harris, *Groton Heights*, 78.
41. Caulkins, *History of New London*, 556. Historian Thomas Farnham notes that a similar situation occurred during Tryon's raid on New Haven in July 1779, where "the British were in no way connected with much of the destroyed or stolen." See Farnham, 38-39.
42. *Norwich Packet*, September 13, 1781.
43. *Connecticut Gazette*, September 14, 1781.
44. Sabine, *Biographical Sketches*, 2:39. During the expedition, Lyman made a detailed map of the harbor, which among other things, clearly establishes the outlines of Forts Griswold, Trumbull, and Nonsense, and locates the positions held by the various units in the raid. See Lyman Map, Sir Henry Clinton Papers, Clements Library.
45. Hempsted narrative in Harris, *Groton Heights*, 66-67.
46. Caulkins, *History of New London*, 552. A complete list of the buildings destroyed and their owners was printed in the *Connecticut Gazette* on October 12, 1781.
47. MacKenzie, *Diary*, 2:626.
48. *Norwich Packet*, October 11, 1781. There seems little reason to doubt the truth of this part of Arnold's report. On September 13 the Packet reported: "The enemy having placed proper guards round the town, they next proceeded, agreeable to orders, to set fire to the stores and shipping; the wind being something high, soon communicated it to the dwelling houses..."
49. Caulkins, *History of New London*, 556.
50. James Lawrence Chew, "An Account of the Old Houses of New London," *Records and Papers of the New London County Historical Society*, Vol. 1, 1890-1894, 79, 82.
51. Caulkins, 556.
52. Caulkins, *History of New London*, 552. This cemetery is located near the corner of present day Hempstead and Richards Streets. Among those buried there are Capt Adam Shapley, commander of Fort Trumbull, and Lt. Richard Chapman, second in command at Fort Trumbull, both casualties of the action at Fort Griswold.
53. Isaac N. Arnold, *The Life of Benedict Arnold: His Patriotism and His Treason* (Chicago: A. C. McClurg and Co., 1897), 354. Jael killed Sisera, commander of the Canaanite army, by pounding a tent pin through his head while he slept. See Judges 4:17-22. In 1854 David Huntington painted a portrait of Abigail Hinman at the moment of this alleged incident entitled Grandmother with a Gun. The painting now hangs in the Lyman Allyn Museum in New London.
54. Caulkins, 553.
55. *Ibid.*, 554.
56. Shaw was not in New London at the time of the raid. He and some friends were fishing off Montauk, and saw the enemy fleet approaching, but it was too late to put into shore. To escape capture, they ran into a nearby creek and waited out the attack. The Shaw Mansion today houses the New London County Historical Society. See "The Shaw Mansion: Connecticut's Naval Office at New London During the War of the American Revolution," Pamphlet, printed by the Society.
57. Caulkins, *History of New London*, 554.
58. *Connecticut Gazette*, October 12, 1781.
59. *Ibid.*, September 7, 1781.

Chapter III

1. Barber, *Connecticut Historical Collections,* 312. The information recorded by Barber on events in Groton was based on the recollections of Joshua Baker and Capt. Elijah Bailey, two survivors of the battle.
2. Harris, *Groton Heights,* 262. Stephen Hempstead, in his 1826 narrative of the battle, claimed that Ledyard received assurances of immediate aid with two or three hundred men from Col. Benadam Gallup. Hempstead narrative in Harris, 49. But Avery Downer, a physician from Preston who treated the wounded after the battle, claimed that "Colonel Benadam Gallup was in the fort previous to the action. Col. Ledyard requested him to go back as far as Capt. Belton's and urge on the men, but before he had time to return the enemy were so near that he could not re-enter the fort." Downer narrative in Harris, 87.
3. For the 35 cannon in the fort and its batteries, there were only 67 "filled cartridges" remaining after the battle according to the British report compiled by Captain J. Lemoine of the Royal Artillery. Colonel Ledyard suffered from no similar lack of musket cartridges, as 10,000 were captured after the battle. See Captain Lemoine's report in MacKenzie, *Diary,* 2:628.
4. Harris, *Groton Heights,* 266-273.
5. Stephen Hempstead narrative in Harris, *Groton Heights,* 48. Hempstead is perhaps the best known member of the garrison besides Col. Ledyard. His 1826 narrative of the battle, though full of embellishments, is still useful to historians. This 27 year old dock worker from New London came from a long line of Hempsteads in the community. Earlier in the war he had attracted notice as the close friend of Captain Nathan Hale, in whose company he had served as first sergeant. Hempstead became a confirmed admirer of Hale after being beaten by him in a wrestling match. See Corey Ford, *A Peculiar Service* (Boston: Little, Brown and Co., 1965), 47-48.
6. MacKenzie, *Diary,* 2:624. Historian Mary Beth Baker also questions Hempstead's reliability as a witness, noting inconsistencies in his account of his relationship with his friend Nathan Hale. As one example, Baker notes Hempstead's claim that he was waiting in Connecticut for Hale to return from his New York mission at the same time that he had been wounded in the Battle of Harlem Heights. "Hempstead seems to have been at two places at the same time." See Mary Beth Baker, *Foundations of Fame: American Amnesia, Nathan Hale and John Andre,* 12. Publication pending.
7. Charles Burr Todd, "The Massacre at Fort Griswold," 166. This ledge of rocks now forms the eastern boundary of the Ledyard Cemetery in Groton.
8. Avery narrative in Harris, *Groton Heights,* 32. Captain Beckwith, an aide-de-camp to General Knyphausen, and a volunteer on this expedition, was best known for his role in the reorganization of General Clinton's intelligence service. During the spring of 1780, while John Andre was away with Clinton in South Carolina, he had conducted secret correspondence with the future traitor, Benedict Arnold. See Mark M. Boatner, *Encyclopedia of the American Revolution* (New York: David McKay Company, Inc., 1966), 65-66.
9. Rogers, *Sesquicentennial of the Battle of Groton Heights,* 26.
10. MacKenzie, *Diary,* 2:624.
11. The disposition of the troops, and the location of cannon, are clearly outlined in Alexander Gray's Sketch, Clinton Papers, Clements Library. See also the diagram of Griswold in Harris, *Groton Heights,* 172.
12. Harris, *Groton Heights,* 234.
13. *Ibid.,* 33.
14. Harris, *Groton Heights,* 48-51; William Latham to Governor Trumbull, no date, Trumbull Papers, CSL. Lt. Chapman was second in command of

Latham's Matross Company, and was the uncle of young Jonathan Brooks, of New London.

15. *Norwich Packet*, September 13, 1781. No British accounts of this incident have come to light. It seems likely that at least some of the British were deceived in view of the following statement by Lt. Obadiah Perkins: "...they fired a Volley into the Air, gave a cheer, and appeared Pleased with the Massacre, and one of them said every Man ought to be put to the sword, for (says he) this is a propur storm, and you fought us after your Colours were struck, the Deponent replied they were not struck, but cut away with your shott, he said 'that might be'"…. Deposition, Lt. Obadiah Perkins to Samuel Mott, April 11, 1782, Trumbull Papers, CSL.

16. MacKenzie, *Diary*, 2:625.

17. Barber, *Connecticut Historical Collections*, 313.

18. Rufus Avery narrative in Harris, *Groton Heights*, 33.

19. Deposition, William Latham to Samuel Mott, April 11, 1782, Trumbull Papers, CSL.

20. Stephen Hempstead to Governor Trumbull, September 30, 1781, Trumbull Papers, CSL.

21. Alexander Gray Sketch, Clinton Papers, Clements Library. Gray was promoted to Lieutenant on September 8, 1781. See *Rivington's Royal Gazette*, September 29, 1781.

22. Deposition, Daniel Eldridge to Samuel Mott, April 12, 1782, Trumbull Papers, CSL.

23. Harris, *Groton Heights*, 221.

24. *Ibid.*, 262.

25. *Ibid.*, 239.

26. See Arnold's report, MacKenzie, *Diary*, 2:626. According to Captain John Peebles, the 40th Regiment had just returned to New York on August 31st [from duty in the Carribbean] and were "very weak not above 250, but they are order'd to get all their Recruits that were drafted into other Regts." As the British reported a strength of 325 for the regiment during the New London expedition, at least 75 men (or nearly a fourth of the unit) were new recruits with no experience serving under the unit's company or regimental commanders. See Peebles, 469.

27. William Heath, *Memoirs of Major General William Heath* (New York: Arno Press, Inc., 1968), 284.

28. *Norwich Packet*, September 13, 1781; Avery narrative in Harris, *Groton Heights*, 37.

29. Caulkins, *History of New London*, 564.

30. MacKenzie, *Diary*, 2:627. The 40th Regiment suffered 86 casualties of 325 men engaged, and the 54th suffered 94 casualties of 441 men engaged. The loss among ranking officers in the 40th was particularly high. In addition to Major Montgomery, Ensign Archibald Whillock was killed outright, and Captain George Craigie, Lt. H. William Smyth, and Ensign Thomas Hyde died of their wounds within a few hours. Among officers of the 54th, Lt. Colonel Eyre and four others (Captain Richard Powell, Lt. Thomas Daunt, Ensign William Rainsforth, and "Volunteer" James Boyd) were wounded, but recovered. The Yagers and the 3rd Battalion of the New Jersey Volunteers suffered no losses, the latter because they did not reach the scene of the action until the close of the battle.

31. Downer narrative in Harris, *Groton Heights*, 85.

32. On January 10, 1782, the following resolve was passed by the Connecticut Assembly: "Upon the memorial of Adam Shapley and Wm. Latham on behalf of themselves and the surviving Officers and Soldiers belonging to. . .Fort Trumbull and Fort Griswold Praying to have their several losses in wearing apparel, Side

Arms, Fusees and Money on the 6th Day of Sept. last...made up to them...Resolved...that the committee of Pay-Table settle and adjust the Accounts of Losses." *Connecticut State Records*, 4:41-42.

33. Charles Allyn Notes, New London County Historical Society, New London, Connecticut.

34 . W. H. Starr, *A Centennial Historical Sketch of the Town of New London* (New London, Connecticut: George Starr, 1876), p. 26.

35. Burned in Groton: 1 school House, 4 barns, 2 shops, 2 stores, and 12 houses. *Connecticut Gazette*, October 13, 1781.

36. Hempstead to Trumbull, September 30, 1781, Trumbull Papers, CSL. Besides Hempstead, the other wounded in the wagon were Amos Lester, Obadiah Perkins, Capt. Shapley, Nathan Moor, Andrew Gallup, Daniel Stanton, Jr. and Joseph Moxley, Jr. Captain Shapley died of his wounds on February 14, 1782 at the age of 43.

37. Avery narrative in Harris, *Groton Heights*, 41.

38. Charles Allyn Notes, New London County Historical Society.

39. Letter to Governor Trumbull, September 10, 1781, Mss., CSL.

40. Deposition, John O. Miner, Miscellaneous Mss., CHS. The Avery House is still to be seen on the grounds of Fort Griswold State Park, where it was moved from its original site, and restored, in 1973.

41. Charles Allyn Notes, New London County Historical Society.

42. Harris, *Groton Heights*, 54-55.

43. Mary P. Root, ed., *Chapter Sketches: Connecticut Daughters of the American Revolution: Patron Saints* (New Haven, CT: Connecticut Chapters, D.A.R., 1901), 356-357.

44. Harris, *Groton Heights*, 55.

45. Letter to Governor Trumbull, September 7, 1781, Trumbull Papers, CHS; MacKenzie, *Diary*, 2:629.

46. Clinton's report in *Rivington's Royal Gazette*, September 22, 1781.

47. Clinton, *American Rebellion*, 563.

48. William B. Willcox, *Portrait of a General: Sir Henry Clinton in the War of Independence* (New York: Alfred A. Knopf, 1964), 422-423. In the Battle off the Chesapeake Capes on September 5, 1781, the French fleet of Admiral DeGrasse defeated a British fleet under Admiral Graves. This victory clearly gave the French naval superiority, and enabled them to cut off Cornwallis from all supplies and reinforcements. From this point on, his fate was sealed.

49. *Rivington's Royal Gazette*, September 22, 1781.

50. Wallace, *Traitorous Hero*, 283.

Chapter IV

1. Hempstead narrative in Harris, *Groton Heights*, 52. Three different officers have been charged with the murder of Ledyard: Captain George Beckwith, Captain Stephen Bromfield, and Lt. Col. Abraham Van Buskirk. Buskirk was clearly not on the scene until after the battle was over, and there is no clear evidence to point to the other two. The mystery will probably remain unsolved.

2. Deposition, Stephen Hempstead to Samuel Mott, April 11, 1782, Trumbull Papers, CSL.

3. Hempstead to Trumbull, September 30, 1781, Trumbull Papers, CSL.

4. Deposition, Hempstead to Mott, April 11, 1782, Trumbull Papers, CSL.

5. Downer narrative in Harris, *Groton Heights*, 86-87.

6. Charles Allyn Notes, New London County Historical Society.

7. Avery narrative in Harris, *Groton Heights*, 35.

8. Rufus Avery to Governor Trumbull, no date, Trumbull Papers, CSL.

9. Deposition, Hempstead to Mott, April 11, 1782, Trumbull Papers, CSL.
10. Thomas Mumford to Governor Trumbull, September 9, 1781, Trumbull Papers, CSL.
11. This information was obtained through the courtesy of the Connecticut Historical Society, Hartford, Connecticut, where the author first made an examination of the garment in August 1974. In 1981 the Society loaned Ledyard's shirt and vest to the Monument House museum in Groton, where it remained on exhibit along with Ledyard's sword for several weeks during the Bicentennial observance in September. This was apparently the first time all three items had been displayed together since leaving the family in the mid-19th century.
12. Governor Trumbull to Thomas Mumford, September 8, 1781, Trumbull Papers, CHS.
13. Samuel F. Wilson, *History of the American Revolution with a Preliminary View of the Character and Principles of the Colonists and their Controversies with Great Britain* (Baltimore, MD: Cushing and Sons, 1834), 338-339.
14. Harris concluded from his examination of the garment that Ledyard was stabbed in the side by a subaltern's sword.
15. *Connecticut Gazette*, September 14, 1781.
16. Hempstead to Trumbull, September 30, 1781, Trumbull Papers, CSL.
17. Captain William Latham to Governor Trumbull, no date, Trumbull Papers, CSL.
18. *Connecticut State Records*, 4:12.
19. Deposition, Obadiah Perkins to Samuel Mott, April 11, 1782, Trumbull Papers, CSL.
20. Avery to Trumbull, no date, Trumbull Papers, CSL.
21. Avery narrative in Harris, *Groton Heights*, 40-41.
22. Hempstead narrative in Harris, 53.54.
23. Barber, *Connecticut Historical Collections*, 313-314.
24. Judges 5:18.

Appendix

1. Frederick MacKenzie, *Diary of Frederick MacKenzie*, Vol. 2 (Cambridge, MA: Harvard University Press, 1930), 624-628.

BIBLIOGRAPHY

I. Manuscripts

Ann Arbor, Michigan. University of Michigan. William L. Clements Library.
Sir Henry Clinton Papers.

Ann Arbor, Michigan. University of Michigan. William L. Clements Library.
Frederick Mackenzie Papers.

Hartford, Connecticut. Connecticut Historical Society. Governor Jonathan
Trumbull Papers.

New London, Connecticut. New London County Historical Society. Charles
Allyn Notes.

II. Diaries, Memoirs and Correspondence

Clinton, Henry. *The American Rebellion: Sir Henry Clinton's Narrative of His
Campaigns, 1775-1782, With an Appendix of Original Documents.* Ed.
William B. Willcox. New Haven, CT: Yale University Press, 1954.

Graves, Thomas. *The Graves Papers and Other Documents Relating to the Naval Operations of the Yorktown Campaign: July to October, 1781.* Ed.
French Ensor Chadwick. New York: Naval History Society, 1916.

Heath, William. *Memoirs of Major General William Heath.* New York: Arno
Press, Inc., 1968.

Mackenzie, Frederick. *Diary of Frederick Mackenzie: Giving a daily narrative
of his military service as an officer of the regiment of Royal Welsh Fusiliers
during the years 1775-1781 in Massachusetts, Rhode Island and New York.*
2 vols. Cambridge, MA: Harvard University Press, 1930.

Peebles, John. *John Peeble's American War: The Diary of a Scottish Grenadier,
1776-1782.* Ed. Ira D. Gruber. Mechanicsburg, PA: Stackpole Books,
1998.

Smith, William. *Historical Memoirs From 26 August 1778 to 12 November 1783
of William Smith: Historian of the Province of New York: Member of the
Governor's Council, and Last Chief Justice of that Province under the Crown:
Chief Justice of Quebec.* Ed. William H. W. Sabine. New York: Arno
Press, 1971.

III. Public Documents

Clark, William Bell, ed. *Naval Documents of the American Revolution.* 6 vols.
Washington, D.C.: Government Printing Office, 1964-1970.

Hoadly, Charles J. *The Public Records of the Colony of Connecticut.* 15 vols.

Hartford, CT: Case, Lockwood and Brainard Col., 1890.

Hoadly, Charles J., and Leonard Woods Labaree, eds. *The Public Records of the State of Connecticut.* 4 vols. Hartford, CT: Case, Lockwood and Brainard Co., 1894-1942.

IV. Newspapers

The Connecticut Gazette and Universal Intelligencer (New London), August to October, 1781.

The Norwich Packet (Norwich, Connecticut), August to October, 1781.

Rivington's Royal Gazette (New York), September, 1781.

V. Secondary Works

Arnold, Isaac N. *The Life of Benedict Arnold: His Patriotism and His Treason.* Chicago: A. C. McClurg and Co., 1897.

Bakeless, John. *Turncoats, Traitors and Heroes.* Philadelphia: J. B. Lippincott Company, 1959.

Barber, John W. *Connecticut Historical Collections: Containing a General Collection of Interesting Facts, Traditions, Biographical Sketches, Anecdotes, etc. Relating to the History and Antiquities of Every Town in Connecticut, with Geographical Descriptions.* New Haven, CT: B. L. Hamlen, 1836.

Boatner, Mark M. *Encyclopedia of the American Revolution.* New York: David McKay Company, Inc., 1966.

Caulkins, Francis M. *History of New London, Connecticut.* New London, CT: Published by the Author, 1852.

Dwight, Timothy. *Travels in New England and New York.* 4 vols. Cambridge, MA: Harvard University Press, 1969.

Ford, Corey. *A Peculiar Service.* Boston: Little, Brown and Company, 1965.

Harris, William W. *The Battle of Groton Heights: A Collection of Narratives, Official Reports, Records, etc. of the Storming of Fort Griswold, the Massacre of its Garrison, and the burning of New London By British Troops under the Command of Brig. Gen. Benedict Arnold, on the Sixth of Sept., 1781.* Rev. Charles Allyn. New London, CT: Charles Allyn, 1882.

Katcher, Philip R. N., *Encyclopedia of British, Provincial and German Army Units, 1775-1783.* Harrisburg, PA: Stackpole Books, 1973.

Leiby, Adrian C. *The Revolutionary War in the Hackensack Valley: The Jersey Dutch and the Neutral Ground 1775-1783.* New Brunswick, NJ: Rutgers University Press, 1962.

Malone, Dumas, ed. *Dictionary of American Biography.* 22 vols. New York: Charles Scribner's Sons, 1928-1944.

Martin, James Kirby. *Benedict Arnold, Revolutionary Hero: An American Warrior Reconsidered.* New York: New York University Press, 1997.

Mather, Frederic Gregory. *The Refugees of 1776 from Long Island to Connecticut.* Albany, NY: J. B. Lyon Co., 1913.

Middlebrook, Louis F. *History of Maritime Connecticut During the American Revolution 1775-1783.* 2 vols. Salem, MA: The Essex Institute, 1925.

Paullin, Charles Oscar. *The Navy of the American Revolution: Its Administra-*

tion, its Policy, and its Achievements. Cleveland. OH: The Burrows Bros. Co., 1906.

Rogers, Ernest E. *Connecticut's Naval Office at New London During the War of the American Revolution.* New London, CT: New London County Historical Society, 1933.

_____, ed. *Sesquicentennial of the Battle of Groton Heights and the Burning of New London, Connecticut: September 6 and 7, 1931.* New London, CT: Fort Griswold and Groton Monument Commission, 1931.

Root, Mary P., ed. *Chapter Sketches; Connecticut Daughters of the American Revolution: Patron Saints.* New Haven, CT: Connecticut Chapters, D.A.R., 1901.

Sabine, Lorenzo. *Biographical Sketches of Loyalists of the American Revolution.* 2 vols. Port Washington, NY: Kennikat Press, Inc., 1966.

Smith, Carolyn, and Helen Vergason. *September 6, 1781: North Groton's Story.* New London, CT: New London Printers, 1981.

Starr, W. H. *A Centennial Historical Sketch of the Town of New London.* New London, CT: George Starr, 1876.

Van Dusen, Albert E. *Connecticut.* New York: Random House, 1961.

Van Tyne, Claude Halstead. *The Loyalists in the American Revolution.* New York: The MacMillan Co., 1902.

Walker, Paul K. *Engineeers of Independence: A Documentary History of the Army Engineers in the American Revolution, 1775-1783.* Washington, D.C.: Government Printing Office, 1981.

Wallace, Willard M. *Traitorous Hero: The Life and Fortunes of Benedict Arnold.* New York: Harper and Bros., 1954.

Ward, Christopher. *The War of the Revolution.* 2 vols. New York: The MacMillan Co., 1952.

Willcox, William B. *Portrait of a General: Sir Henry Clinton in the War of Independence.* New York: Alfred A. Knopf, 1964.

Wilson, Samuel F. *History of the American Revolution with a Preliminary View of the Character and Principles of the Colonists and their Controversies with Great Britain.* Baltimore, MD: Cushing and Sons, 1834.

VI. Journal Articles

Baker, Mary E. "Foundations of Fame: American Amnesia, Nathan Hale and John Andre." Publication pending.

Chew, James Lawrence. "An Account of the Old Houses of New London." *Records and Papers of the New London County Historical Society.* Vol. I (1890-1894), Part IV, 77-96.

Farnham, Thomas. "The Day the Enemy Was In Town: The British Raids on Connecticut, July 1779." *Journal of The New Haven Colony Historical Society.* Vol. 24, No. 2 (Summer 1976), 3-63.

Todd, Charles Burr. "The Massacre at Fort Griswold." *Magazine of American History.* 7 (September 1881): 161-174.

ABOUT THE AUTHOR

Dr. Walter L. Powell is the Historic Preservation Officer for the Borough of Gettysburg, and Co-Director of the Historic Preservation Program at Sheperd College in Sheperdstown, West Virginia. A native of Connecticut, Dr. Powell has written and lectured widely on Connecticut's role in the American Revolution and Civil War. He lives in Gettysburg with his wife Susan and children Nathaniel and Sarah Ellen.

THOMAS PUBLICATIONS publishes books about the American Colonial era, the Revolutionary War, the Civil War, and other important topics. For a complete list of titles, please visit our web site, www.thomaspublications.com.

Or write to:

THOMAS PUBLICATIONS
P.O. Box 3031
Gettysburg, PA 17325